DUR

G000123278

IN OLD PHOTOGRAPHS

DISTANT AND AERIAL VIEWS of Durham reveal the splendour of its site and the contrasts to be found within. The vista from Observatory Hill is one of the most famous views of the city. Observatory Hill also affords good tobogganing when conditions are suitable, though this treat has been denied to local children in recent years because of mild winters.

DURHAM
IN OLD PHOTOGRAPHS

COLLECTED BY
JUNE CROSBY

ALAN SUTTON

Alan Sutton Publishing Limited
Phoenix Mill · Far Thrupp · Stroud · Gloucestershire

First published 1990

British Library Cataloguing in Publication Data

Durham in old photographs
1. Durham (County). Durham, history
I. Crosby, J.H. (June Hilda)
942.8'65

ISBN 0-86299-617-1

Typeset in 9/10 Korinna.
Typesetting and origination by
Alan Sutton Publishing Limited.
Printed in Great Britain by
The Bath Press, Avon.

CONTENTS

THE PENINSULA FROM THE AIR, C. 1938. A magnificent view from the album of the late J. Landt Mawson, which demonstrates better than any words the natural defences of Durham and the dominance of the cathedral, guarded by the castle at its weakest point. Compare it with the map of 1595 on p.143; the photograph was probably taken by Miss Christopher, Principal of St Hild's College, Durham, 1910–33.

INTRODUCTION

A rough shelter of boughs was erected over the coffin of St Cuthbert of Lindisfarne on a rocky plateau 100 ft above the river Wear at Dunholm in about AD 994. From this simple structure developed the City of Durham which will soon celebrate its first thousand years and which has been described as the finest city in western Europe.

After his death in AD 687 St Cuthbert's grave became a place of pilgrimage and, as a result of the miracles associated with him, many gifts of land and money were given to the Lindisfarne community as custodians of the saint. In 875 Viking raids forced the monks to move to the mainland for safety but they did not lose their estates and power for they took St Cuthbert's body with them — the outward symbol of their authority throughout Northumbria. By the time St Cuthbert's Community moved to Dunholm their wealth and influence had increased and 'St Cuthbert's patrimony' extended over most of the land of the three rivers — the Tyne, Wear and Tees.

The new city prospered. By 1017 there was a small, walled city on the Peninsula with a stone minster to house the shrine of St Cuthbert; a civil settlement lay to the north of the church and the houses of the community. Durham was admirably placed as the administrative centre of the lands held in St Cuthbert's name and its defensive worth had been proven when the city repulsed a Scottish attack in 1006.

The Norman invasion of 1066 threatened the stability of the city but the power, privileges and possessions of St Cuthbert were recognized by the Normans. Durham's strategic position plus the administrative framework already established gave the Normans a ready-made power base for controlling the area and for dealing with border troubles with the Scots. However, between 1071 and 1093 the old community was taken over and completely reformed by Norman officers. The last Northumbrian leader of the community was replaced by a Norman, Bishop Walcher. In 1082 the remaining members of the old community were replaced by monks of the strict Benedictine order and services were also brought into line with Benedictine liturgy. In 1093 the minster was demolished and work begun on what was to be the finest Romanesque cathedral in Europe.

The city too was transformed under Norman influence. The castle was begun in 1072. In c. 1100 Bishop Flambard cleared the Palace Green area of houses, thus making the Peninsula purely an ecclesiastical and military zone. Some of the dispossessed inhabitants probably moved into the Market Place which was already inhabited, but most went across the river to Crossgate and Framwellgate. Framwellgate Bridge was built to link the inner and outer settlements. This bridge was to be the only approach to the city from the south-west until the mid-twentieth century. In c. 1180 Bishop du Puiset ordered the building of Elvet Bridge which stimulated settlement in the Elvets. The granting of a market charter to the citizens in 1179 confirmed the city as the region's trade centre. The road from the Market Place to the twin ports of Bishop and Monk Wearmouth encouraged settlement north-eastwards along Claypath and Gilesgate. The walls encircling the Peninsula were extended to include the market and the city was approached by four guarded gates on two bridges, at the Clayport and at the Watergate in South Bailey.

Thus by c. 1200 the outline plan and street pattern of Durham was established by geographical factors and the planning decisions of the early Norman bishops. There was no truly major alteration to the overall plan until 1831 when North Road was created. Even when the relief roads of the mid-twentieth century were built most of the medieval street pattern remained intact. This is one of the factors contributing to the unique character of Durham.

The wealth and power of the Bishops of Durham and the importance of St Cuthbert's shrine as a place of pilgrimage made medieval Durham a prosperous city and gave it a character still evident today. It was a cathedral city, a centre of learning, a place of pilgrimage, a county town, an administrative centre and the trading centre for its hinterland. The cathedral is still a place of pilgrimage; the university has replaced the monastery as the centre of learning, and occupies much of the peninsula; and the city is still a county capital and administrative centre. Durham still has a market and serves as a shopping centre for local villages as it has done for centuries. Even in the medieval period Durham trade was very local as there was no navigable waterway to encourage a mercantile class as found at York or Newcastle.

In spite of the changes of many centuries and the advent of the railway and the motor car Durham retains its medieval imprint. The cathedral and castle dominate the skyline; the medieval streets still survive as do many of the vennels. The long views of cathedral and castle are visually the most exciting views in Europe. From one direction one sees these great buildings soaring above the pleasant rural setting of the river and its wooded banks; from another viewpoint they are to be seen in their urban setting above the uneven roof tops of the small city humbly sheltering beneath their protection.

The rich legacy has, however, caused problems for late-twentieth-century Durham. The streets of the city were not designed for modern traffic; yet to destroy them would be to mutilate this city and the new roads of the 1960s only partially solved the problem.

The delights of Durham are being discovered by an ever-increasing number of visitors and would-be commuters who wish to live in such a place. Developers also discovered the city's possibilities during the property boom of the 1970s; the results have not been auspicious. The special qualities of Durham – the cathedral and castle on the rock encircled by the lovely river and its banks; the still recognizably medieval layout of the city clustered below; the green belt reaching right into the heart of the city – these are worth preserving. Yet a city is a living thing where people live, work and enjoy their leisure, so Durham cannot be 'frozen' for posterity but rather has to change according to the needs of its inhabitants. There has been much continuity together with many changes, as the illustrations in this book will demonstrate. The photographs deal only with the inner, historic City of Durham – the present conservation area. It is hoped that justice will be done in a second Durham volume to the later development of the city and to the interesting villages such as Pittington and Witton Gilbert which became part of the city in the reorganization of 1974.

SECTION ONE

The City
on the Rock

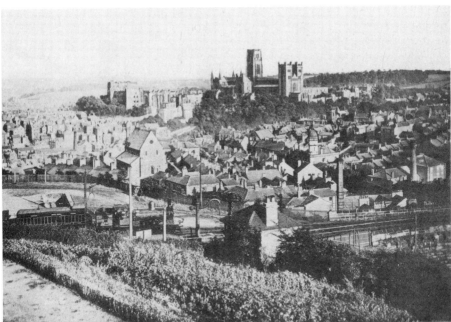

'RUSKIN'S VIEW' – so called because John Ruskin was so entranced by this vista of the city. This photograph was on a chocolate box about fifty-five years ago. It was already out of date then for it shows Robson's mill and its chimney stack (at the right) and St Godric's Church without the tower which was added in 1909. It is the view seen from the railway station and Wharton Park.

AN AERIAL VIEW of the Peninsula in 1938. The cathedral dominates the scene, dwarfing the castle, the viaduct and St Oswald's Church. The trees massed around the Peninsula define the loop of the river. Many of the fields in the far distance have been built upon since the Second World War, especially those to the right of old Framwellgate snaking its way up the hill to Aykley Heads (in the top right corner). The straight line of Church Street running past St Oswald's was an unfenced green lane in the eighteenth century, yet it was 'The London Road'. (Mrs J. Stobbs)

AN AERIAL VIEW of the cathedral complex looking north towards the castle, 1938. On the left is Framwellgate Bridge and on the right Elvet Bridge. The former Paradise Gardens lie just beyond Elvet Bridge. St Nicholas' Church is at top centre; to the left the massed buildings of the carpet factory line the riverside and to the right the curve of Claypath can be clearly seen. The photograph shows how the city's historic core is contained in a surprisingly small area. A sixteenth-century antiquary claimed a longbow could be fired from the river banks right over the Peninsula to the far bank of the river on the other side with ease. (Mrs J. Stobbs)

THE WESTERN TOWERS OF THE CATHEDRAL. This is the view which dramatically confronts visitors as they walk up Owengate and Palace Green opens out before them. The cathedral garth still has its railings and the road is still unpaved. The picture cannot be later than 1915 as the iron grille, installed at the cathedral's north door in that year because of a rumour that the suffragettes were planning to damage the interior, is not in place.

THE COURTYARD, DURHAM CASTLE, c. 1900. The portico on the left flanked by twin Ionic columns was erected by Bishop Cosin, whose coat of arms surmounts the pediment. Cosin was also responsible for the four full-height buttresses topped by ogee-shaped helmets. The buttresses support the Great Hall built by Bishop Bek in about 1300 over the Norman undercroft and still in use though altered and restored. The Great Hall has always provided a splendid setting for ceremonial occasions. Perhaps the most significant was the banquet given by Bishop Fox in 1503 in honour of Princess Margaret Tudor, on her way to marry James IV of Scotland. Her descendant, James VI, became King of England in 1603 and so united the two countries.

THE TUNSTALL CHAPEL, the castle, (1909), named after Cuthbert Tunstall, bishop for thirty-seven years under Henry VIII, Edward VI, Mary Tudor, and into Elizabeth I's reign. During his episcopacy St Cuthbert's shrine was dismantled and the monastery suppressed. He was briefly deprived of his see by Edward, but re-instated by Mary. When Elizabeth became queen she placed him under house arrest and refused to have him take part in her coronation. Yet he died peacefully at the then great age of eighty-five. One can only hope that he found solace in his castle chapel. His east window (above) remains, but the chapel was enlarged by Cosin and Crewe. The sixteenth-century choir stalls were originally in Bishop Auckland Palace Chapel; a few have their misericords, including one of a man wheeling his bad-tempered wife in a wheelbarrow. (Mrs J. Stobbs)

ALTHOUGH THE CASTLE became University College in 1837 there was not a total surrender of the premises to the new university. Bishop Maltby retained a suite of rooms for the use of the Bishops and their servants, and apartments were also needed for the judges on assize. The judges were accustomed to having the use of fourteen rooms but a compromise was reached; the judges were allocated four bedrooms in the castle and a house in Queen Street for their retinue. This is one of those rooms with ornate fireplace, tapestry hangings and even a pole screen for protection should the fire be too fierce.

THIS RICHLY ORNAMENTED DOOR was originally the ceremonial entrance to the hall of Hugh du Puiset, bishop from 1153 to 1195, and would have been approached by an exterior staircase. It became an interior door when Bishop Tunstall erected a two-storey extension in front of the earlier building, and at some unknown date it was plastered over and forgotten until the early nineteenth century, when it was rediscovered. The upper mouldings of the doorway were in near pristine condition while the jambs were weathered; this suggested that the vanished staircase had been roofed but had had open sides.

CASTLE BATTERY AND ST CUTHBERT'S CHEST – so the caption reads, but it is buttery not battery and the ancient iron-bound chest was not St Cuthbert's. The buttery, used for storing bread and ale and other food as well as butter, was created by partitioning off the southern end of the Great Hall. It was installed by Bishop Fox; his badge, 'a pelican in her piety' (i.e., a pelican feeding her young with her blood), and '1499 Est Deo Gracia' are carved above the large serving hatches which pierce the distinctive black-and-white screen.

INVESTIGATING THE OLD WELL in the courtyard of the castle, c. 1932. Castles were built to withstand siege and a supply of water close at hand was essential. The castle was so much in need of repair that for about five years before major rescue work began in 1931 the building was 'unsafe for a large assembly' and Convocation and other big meetings were held elsewhere. A Durham Castle Preservation Trust was set up in 1928 and its fund-raising efforts, together with a grant from the Pilgrim Trust, enabled the necessary works to go ahead. (Durham University Library)

NURSE CROWDY, MISS STANLEY, MRS GRICE AND MISS CHRISTMAS all worked at Aubrey House, near London, when it was a nursing home for men wounded in the First World War. They had a holiday in Durham as guests of the Mawson family in 1918. Here they are walking across Palace Green past the Diocesan Registry, which was erected in 1820. The sixteenth-century doorway at the right of this building belonged to the old County Court House, demolished in 1811. (Mrs J. Stobbs)

MUSEUM SQUARE, NORTH BAILEY. There were many such yards until the 1960s. Moody's Buildings, Souter's Yard and Hutton's Buildings are examples; but most have now gone. Museum Square vanished in 1973. Its name was acquired when the University Museum was moved here in 1847 as its first location (the disused Fulling Mill) was too damp. A fine collection of artefacts and a remarkable collection of stuffed birds were assembled; but they were dispersed during the First World War and much was not recovered. A great auk, thought by many to be the rarest exhibit, was sold in the 1970s. (Durham University Library)

COSIN'S HALL, PALACE GREEN, an early-eighteenth-century house previously known as Archdeacon's Inn. It had been subdivided into two houses by the time the university purchased it around 1840. At first it was used as an overflow for University College but by 1856 was no longer needed. In 1851 a hall of residence was opened for less affluent students in some houses in the Bailey and was known as Cosin's Hall. This little community and its name moved to Palace Green in 1856 but the venture failed and in 1864 the building became part of University College once more. The imposing façade remains but sweeping changes (heralded by this builder's yard on the Green) have altered the interior.

THE CENTRAL TOWER and the north crossing of the cathedral, 1898. This photograph was taken by John Veitch, whose son was a founder member of the city's photographic club. In 1827, Ignatius Bonomi, then cathedral architect, supervised repairs to the tower during which a workman fell from the roof but suffered only severe bruising. A local gossip column gave St Cuthbert the credit for his escape.

THE MASSIVE CHARACTER of the Norman pillars of the cathedral nave is clearly shown in this photograph, also by Veitch. The round pillars are 27 ft high and just under 7 ft in diameter. The spiral, reed, chevron and lozenge are typical Norman patterns, all of which are found in Durham Cathedral; the chevron and the lozenge being illustrated here (together with the compound style of pillar). Before this the patterns were usually painted. At Durham, however, the four patterns were cut into the stone and so were an integral part of the structure. This Durham innovation was quickly imitated elsewhere.

THE SOUTH AISLE of the cathedral nave, looking towards the east end and the Chapel of the Nine Altars. The *quadrapartite-* (i.e., four-branched) vaulting of the roof was a major development in building techniques and it is thought that this style of roofing was first deployed at Durham. The interlaced blind arcading decorating the walls is also thought to be a Durham innovation.

THE CHAPEL OF THE NINE ALTARS in another turn-of-the-century photograph by John Veitch, looking north towards the Joseph window, 'the finest piece of Gothic design at Durham'. The monument beneath the window is of William van Mildert, the last of the 'Prince Bishops'. The soaring pillars are of Frosterly marble, a fossilized limestone found in Weardale and used in many County Durham churches in lieu of true marble. The thirteenth-century builders achieved the great height of this easternmost part of the cathedral by cutting down into the soft subsoil and omitting a crypt so that the floor level is about 9 ft below that of the shrine of St Cuthbert.

THE MONASTIC BUILDINGS at Durham are probably the best and most complete example of the Benedictine layout surviving today. This photograph of the east walk of the early fifteenth-century cloister arcades, with its fine timbered ceiling, looks towards the elaborately decorated late-twelfth-century door into the cathedral. On the right is the door of the chapter house, flanked by two windows (now blocked); the zigzag tooling of the door arches and windows was a design widely used by the Normans; these date from c. 1140.

THE UNDERCROFT OF THE CATHEDRAL, c. 1900. The short, sturdy pillars and ribbed roof support the monks' dormitory above. Before the Dissolution of the monastery the undercroft was divided into three parts – the spendiment, or treasury; the 'great cellar', and the warming house, where the monks could find a little comfort. The treasury survives and now houses many of the cathedral's precious manuscripts. The southern end of the undercroft opened as a restaurant and bookshop in 1975, thus continuing in modern idiom the cathedral's centuries' old traditions of hospitality and learning. The central part is now a small museum displaying relics of St Cuthbert and the famous sanctuary knocker.

THE COLLEGE, C. 1896. The castellated house at the right is the residence of the Lightfoot Professor of Divinity; one former occupant was Michael Ramsey, who later became Archbishop of Canterbury. The house incorporates part of the medieval guest hall; it was given its present appearance in the early nineteenth century, possibly by William Atkinson. Bishop Auckland, born Atkinson, was a protégé of Bishop Barrington and designed Abbotsford for Sir Walter Scott. The two stately figures in the picture were described by its owner as university policemen; they look far too dignified and clerical and are probably the proctors (i.e., the members of staff responsible for student discipline), Revd A. Plummer and Revd J.R. Shortt. The house to the left of the ivy-covered conduit was formerly a clergy residence; it is now part of the Chorister School. The house was 'modernized' in the eighteenth century when a new staircase and the Gibbs style doorway was inserted. Earlier features survive, however, including part of an early-seventeenth-century staircase. (Dean and Chapter Library)

THE FORMER ST MARY'S COLLEGE in 1937. Before central heating was installed, students' rooms had coal fires. The maids, or 'bedders', had to clean out the ashes every day and carry up heavy buckets of coal. The college moved to new buildings in 1952 and this house has been part of the Chorister School ever since.

THIS HIDDEN LITTLE LANE runs between the Bailey and the east end of the former monastic complex; it is approached through the college gateway. It housed the workshops and brewhouse; the former function continues, though not the latter.

SOME OF THE BUILDINGS in the lane shown in the previous photograph were renovated in the late 1960s; this shows one gutted prior to modernization. It revealed the remains of a bread oven.

DUN COW LANE and the west front of St Mary-le-Bow Church. Dun Cow Lane derives its name from the carving of the cow and milkmaid on the cathedral opposite. The building line of the lane is an ancient one: an arch and traces of a newel stair from a twelfth-century gate were uncovered in the near wall a few years ago and left exposed. Lydgate (i.e., the place where coffins rested on their way to burial) was another name for the lane. St Mary-le-Bow became redundant in 1970 and is now a museum and heritage centre and its glorious early-eighteenth-century woodwork is carefully preserved. The blind arch is thought to be part of the room over the medieval gateway which spanned the Bailey until it collapsed in 1671.

IN HIS MEMOIRS William Henderson recalls how his mother remembered sitting in a window seat of a little bay window overlooking Bow Lane listening to the three gifted Porter children read the stories they had written. This (at the left) is said to be that window. Robert became Sir Robert Ker Porter, historical painter to the Czar, and his sisters became fashionable novelists. *Thaddeus of Warsaw* won Jane an award from the exiled Polish community and *The Scottish Chiefs* was a best-seller of the day. Anna Maria was best known for her *Artless Tales*.

ST MARY-LE-BOW CHURCH decorated for Christmas, c. 1900. The pews have since been removed but the fine woodwork of the roodscreen and sanctuary remains (eighteenth century in date though seventeenth century in style). Alongside the church is Bow Lane (pictured in the previous photograph), which led down to a gate in the city walls. In 1450 the monastery closed the lane by locking the gate at the west end of the church but Bishop Neville ordered it to be unlocked. (Durham University Library)

THE INTERIOR OF ST JOHN'S COLLEGE CHAPEL. This tiny Norman church of St Mary-the-Less was built for the men guarding the castle. It has been used by St John's since the college's foundation and was handed over to the college permanently in 1919. Little of the original Norman work remained after the heavy-handed restoration of 1847; but the chancel arch, seen here, survived, together with some bits of zigzag work. A monument to Count Borulawski, designed by J.A. Cory, can be seen in the chapel.

THE STEEPLY SLOPING GARDENS in South Bailey behind St John's College. The Durham Girls' High School was founded in 1884 under the auspices of the Church Schools' Company Ltd, with a local supervisory committee. The school's first premises were at No. 3 South Bailey, previously the home of William Henderson, the carpet manufacturer. Miss Elizabeth Gray was the first headmistress. The school later moved to Leazes House, which had been the home of William Henderson's elder brother and partner, John Henderson, MP. No. 3 South Bailey was taken over by St John's College, which now dominates this stretch of the Bailey.

The University on the Peninsula

NEW GRADUATES leaving Castle Hall after Congregation in 1913. The university was founded in 1832 and is the third oldest English university. Motivation for its foundation came largely from Durham clergy and the Church provided buildings and much of the finance. Not everyone favoured the idea; Mrs Fox of the Bailey bemoaned it and said what an anxiety it would prove to all mothers with daughters.

COSIN'S CLERGY LIBRARY became part of the new university and was used for examinations in the early years. It is now a research library. In 1962 the University Librarian, Mr David Ramage, painted a frieze of poets, law-givers and scientists after the manner of the original seventeenth-century friezes by John Baptist van Eersell.

VERDANT GREEN'S ROOM in the castle, 1921. Henry Bradley occupied this room when a student at University College. He was both an artist and writer, contributing drawings to *Punch* and the *Illustrated London News*. He wrote under the pen-name of Cuthbert Bede and many of his stories were published in *The Girl's Own Paper*. His amusing vignettes, based upon student life in Durham but adapted to Oxford to suit the taste of the reading public, first appeared in the *Illustrated London News* and were later the inspiration for his book *The Adventures of Verdant Green*.

HENRY BRADLEY'S ORIGINAL DRAWINGS, based upon his own experiences as a Durham undergraduate at the castle from 1845 to 1848. At this time the city's only railway station was in Gilesgate (Archibald's now use the buildings which remain for their DIY business). The drawing at the top right shows the 'fresmonne' being jolted down the steep, cobbled hill of Gilesgate upper bank; the raised pavement is clearly indicated. A restless night in The Waterloo in New Elvet dreaming that he 'gets a treble 3rd and is made a bishop' is followed by an interview with the warden – recognizably Archdeacon Thorp. Then he inspects and rejects rooms in University House (later Cosin's Hall). Finally he takes up residence in the castle, though 'dismayed at ye number of steps leading thereto'. (Durham University Library)

A CARTOON from the *The Undergrad* of 1882. Entitled *Don Dunelmo*, it shows Dean Lake, Warden of the University, as the Mikado, surrounded by members of staff.

UNDERGRADUATES LEAVING THE CATHEDRAL after an end-of-term service and prizegiving, c. 1915. Joseph L. Mawson is leaning over the railings at the right. A true 'DBC' (Durham-born citizen), Mr Mawson was a pupil of Durham School and a student at the castle. He served on the Western Front until wounded and invalided out of the army. He became a solicitor and followed his father in serving the diocese from the New Exchequer Buildings in North Bailey. Part of his work concerned the Court of Chancery – the last remnant of the Bishopric's Palatinate privileges, which were abolished in 1971, when it was said that there were records going back over three hundred years in the court building. Unfortunately, when the exchequer became part of the University Law Department some documents were destroyed, though many were saved thanks to the enterprise of Mrs L. Drury and Miss M. McCollum. (Mrs J. Stobbs)

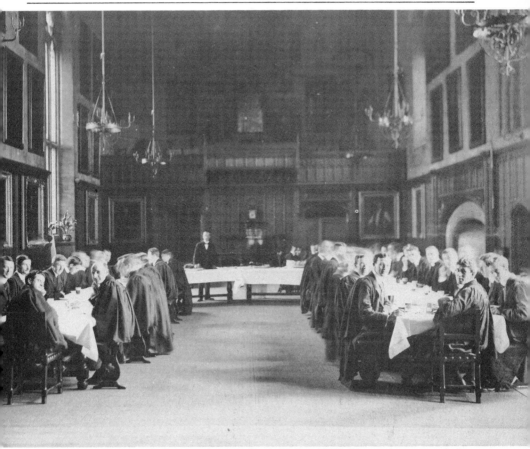

DINING IN HALL: University College students in Castle Hall, c. 1915. The students were so few that they 'rattled about in the ramshackle old building'. The daily routine was very formal; gowns were worn for lectures, church services and college meals. A butler, assisted by servants, presided over meals, which always began and ended with the saying of grace. Freshly starched white linen covered the tables. The master and staff dined on high table, as they still do. (Mrs J. Stobbs)

THE VENERABLE H.W. WATKINS was appointed to the newly founded Chair of Hebrew in 1880, from which he did not retire until 1920, a year before this photograph was taken. He was also a canon of the cathedral and Archdeacon of Durham. He so detested smoking that it was said that not even a bishop dared smoke in front of him; he was also a strict teetotaller. When the First World War began he volunteered his services to the military thus: 'I am seventy years of age, I am called the Venerable, but I can walk twenty miles a day and I can shoot. If you can make any use of me do so.'

THE REVD C.S. WALLIS in St John's College garden, 1921. Wallis, a Durham graduate, became principal in 1919, the year St John's became a university college. It had been founded as St John's Hall following a a Lambeth Conference decision in 1908 to improve clergy training.

UNDERGRADUATES ON PALACE GREEN, 1921. On the left is what was then the University Library; the castle keep is in the background. Then as now students were not supposed to walk across the grass. Academic gowns were worn by students and staff for lectures, cathedral services, and for dining in hall until about 1960.

THE INTERIOR OF HATFIELD COLLEGE CHAPEL, c. 1883. The chapel was built in 1853 to the design of the Revd James Turner, a former architect who began his clerical training at Durham in 1848 and later become Bishop of Grafton and Armidale. At first the chapel 'contained nothing but bare walls and seats, and a small organ that was never used'. A new organ was installed at the west end in 1883.

P.J. HEAWOOD, Professor of Mathematics and Proctor of the University, in his study at High Close in 1921. Professor Emeritus 'Pussy Heawood' was a distinctive figure in post-war Durham in his ancient Aberdeen cape. He delighted in wandering into the university offices in North Bailey to demonstrate that he could add up long lists of figures 'in his head' faster than the adding machines then used by the staff in the office. Through the pages of a learned journal he and a theological colleague conducted a long and heated debate, but they never discussed their differences face to face.

DR F.B. JEVONS, 1921. Frank Byron Jevons served the university for forty-seven years. He became a tutor in classics in 1882; then the first censor of non-collegiate students; Principal of Hatfield College from 1896 to 1923, and Vice-Chancellor from 1910.

CHARLES STEWART HENRY VANE-TEMPEST-STEWART, 7th Marquess of Londonderry, KC, in his robes as Chancellor of the University in 1937, the year the university celebrated the centenary of the charter granted by William IV. Lord Londonderry had a distinguished career. He was MP for Maidstone before entering the House of Lords, and held several senior government posts. He was Mayor of Durham in 1936.

THE FIRST CREW of the University Rowing Club in 1936/7. The cox was C.B.C. Ap Ivor whose lung power was said to be prodigous. Behind him, from left to right, stand M. Gregory, H. Saxby, T. Lowrey and K.W. Puddy.

THE READING-ROOM of the Durham Union Society, 1921. Before the Second World War the Union Society was something akin to a gentleman's club for students, where meals could be ordered at any time and where there was always a plentiful supply of papers and magazines and a place for a quiet pipe or cigar.

MISS ANGEL LAWRENCE, Principal of St Hild's College 1933–51. An excellent debater and ranconteur, she was highly respected by colleagues and students, and wrote a history of the college to mark its centenary in 1958.

An eighteenth-century garden made a lovely haven for students of St Mary's College, the first women's college at the university. Female students were first allowed as early as 1881, but none came as no suitable accommodation or scholarships were offered. Home-based students and four members of St Hild's were admitted in 1896. In 1899 Abbey House on Palace Green was opened as the forerunner of St Mary's and in 1916 Miss R.E. Donaldson was appointed principal of the college, and given this former prebend's residence.

THE UNIVERSITY OBSERVATORY was erected in 1839 to house the collection of astronomical instruments purchased from Dr T.J. Hussey of the Royal Astronomical Society, and to provide a house for the observer. The collection was enlarged during the following decade when the observatory contributed to research which established the exact position of Neptune and several of the asteroids. In 1850 an obelisk was erected by local benefactor J.L. Wharton as a north point for the observatory.

THE NEW COMMON ROOM, St Hild's College, 1904. 'Just seen the interior of the new room added to St Hild's – looks very comfortable. Hope you got home safely' – this was the message written on the back of this photograph sent to Mrs Stoker of Dinnington. To those who had known the spartan routine and furnishings of the college when it was first founded in 1858 the new room was downright luxurious.

River Banks and Bridges

ROBERT BERTRAM'S drawing of the west end of Framwellgate Bridge, c. 1920. Most of the property to the right of the bridge has vanished. This area was known as Five Ways, for Crossgate, South Street, North Road, Framwellgate, and Milburngate converged here. The faded lettering advertising the former Five Ways Hotel was discernible on its walls before its demolition in the mid-1960s.

PARADISE HOUSE, CLAYPATH RIVERSIDE. This is taken from an old photograph of an undated drawing, which must be after 1856 as the spire of the new St Nicholas' Church is shown. Paradise Lane is to the left of the house. Paradise Gardens stretched along the river banks. Most of the gardens were acquired during the 1830s by Gilbert Henderson, the carpet manufacturer, who built Leazes House at the east end of the grounds.

A LOVELY PICTURE of Crook Hall Farm c. 1910, when it was farmed by John Fowler; to the right is part of the eighteenth-century wing of Crook Hall, then held by James Fowler. It is difficult to believe that this 'rural corner' is within sight of Milburngate Bridge; it was a working farm until c. 1960, when the farmer was known for his Landrace boars. The Crook Hall complex of house, farm and mill has a remarkable history traceable from the late twelfth century. There are remains of a moated site and other archaeological 'humps and bumps' still to be investigated, while the building retains a late-fourteenth-century hall which has been carefully rescued from oblivion by Mr and Mrs J. Hagwood under the direction of architect Mr I. Curry. (Durham University Library)

THE EAST END OF ELVET BRIDGE, *c.* 1910. A seventeenth-century antiquary claimed that the bridge had fourteen arches; today we can only see ten – seven 'wet' and three 'dry' arches. These old buildings are the only ones left on the bridge though there is evidence that there were once buildings right across. The smaller building perched on top of the cutwater was formerly the thirteenth-century chapel of St Andrew; a chapel to St James stood at the other end of the bridge. These were for travellers to pray for a safe journey or give thanks for its completion and at the same time make a donation to the church and for the upkeep of the bridge. The carriages are standing behind the Half Moon Inn, where there were livery stables and carriage works.

BATHS BRIDGE UNDER FLOOD, 1 June 1924, with the baths to the right. This iron bridge of 1898 replaced a wooden bridge of 1855 which had been paid for by a public subscription organized by Edward Peele, a local vet, to provide a convenient link between Gilesgate and the Elvets and easier access to the public baths and swimming baths. The baths were designed by John Augustus Cory in 1853 and erected in 1855/6; he installed Egyptian-style pillars around the pool. (Mrs J. Stobbs)

AN AFTERNOON ON THE RIVER, May 1915. White flannels and college blazer were the 'accepted' wear on such occasions. Ideas about dress were far more rigid seventy-five years ago. A contributor to the *University Journal* in 1917 railed against the 'tout cads' of the university who were lowering standards by wearing blazers under academic at a time when men were dying on the Western Front to maintain the standards of western civilization. (Mrs J. Stobbs)

THE EBDON HOME on the river bank near Prebends Bridge. The house, known as 'Count's house' because of the Ebdons' colourful lodger, Count Borulawski, was demolished about a century ago and local folklore has given its popular name to a nearby classical-style garden house. The bridge in the illustration is the old Prebends Bridge destroyed in the great floods of 1771.

THE OLD FULLING MILL, c. 1935. This mill was one of two mills on the banks below the cathedral belonging to the monastery. The corn mill existed before the end of the twelfth century when there was a dispute about it between the monks and Bishop Philip de Poitou. The fulling mill was constructed in about 1416 for £15 0s. 9d. apparently in response to the growth of a small weaving industry in the city. Though it did not prosper, fulling seems to have continued intermittently. By the sixteenth century the two mills were called the Lead Mill (because of its lead roof) and the Jesus Mill. By the 1950s the mill had become a café; it is now a museum of archaeology.

THE RIVER FROM THE RACECOURSE, looking towards Leazes House, a well-proportioned nineteenth-century house built by the Hendersons. For many years it was Durham High School and had several buildings added to it. More recently it was the science block of Bede College. It has been sensitively restored and is now a private house again. A terrace of town houses has been erected in the grounds and enjoys a fine south facing view across the river.

ONE OF THE DELIGHTS OF DURHAM is the opportunity for pleasant walks along the river banks only two or three minutes away from the shops. This photograph was taken in Pimlico, near the head of South Street; the banks above Prebend's Bridge are to the right.

THE FORMER RACE TRACK. 'They say from this city that their races for years to come will be greatly altered and advanced, both in regard to the number of the prizes and their value, and that their course will be new and greatly superior to the two generally used by the said city.' This entry in the *Racing Calendar* of 1733 is the first mention of the race track in Elvet though references to racing in the city occur from 1665. Race meetings continued until 1887 by which time races were held in late April and in July, when they coincided with the miners' Big Meeting. In 1888 the Race Committee surrendered their lease to the university; this meant the closure of the race track and the expulsion of the City Cricket Club from the pitch the committee had sub-leased to them. Although some felt that the races 'had degenerated into a very disreputable affair', and the cricketers were compensated for their eviction, there was considerable ill-feeling in the town towards the university, which lingered for many years. The site is still known as the Racecourse.

A CHARMING STUDY of a part of Kepier Wood, which offers one of the loveliest walks near the centre of a city that has several other beautiful walks nearby. Originally the ancient wood extended much nearer the city but in 1900 there was large-scale felling which left 'an area of complete devastation' according to the *Durham County Advertiser*. 'Nothing was left that was worth a few shillings. In a heavily taxed place like Durham such a scheme might seem Utopian; still we cannot but help in indulging what seems a vain regret – that someone did not intervene to preserve the beauties of Kepier for public enjoyment.' (Mrs J. Stobbs)

RISING ABOVE THE RIVER the gardens of St Hild's College (seen here in 1937) command a magnificent view of the cathedral and castle, a view also enjoyed by its neighbour, the College of the Venerable Bede. Hild's (for women) and Bede (for men) were both church colleges founded in the nineteenth century for the training of teachers. In 1976 they were amalgamated as the College of St Hild and St Bede and in 1979 their distinguished service as training colleges came to an end.

THE MAYOR OF DURHAM, Mrs Margaret Thornhill, presiding over the opening of the new Milburngate Bridge in 1967. Mrs Thornhill's mayoress was her daughter Anne, seen here in a two-tone outfit. Next to her is Mrs S.C. Docking, whose husband, as Chairman of the County Council, formally opened the bridge. Between them is Mr Brockbank, Clerk to the County Council. Next to the Town Clerk, wearing his wig, is Mr McIntyre, who later became mayor. In the background, 'banal yet self-assertive', is the unfinished mass of Milburngate House; being a Crown building no planning permission was required. (Mr D.V. Kelly)

STUDENTS WALKING OVER KINGSGATE BRIDGE, which was completed in 1963 to link university buildings on either side of the river. The innovatory design by Ove Arup and Partners involved the bridge being built in two halves parallel with the river banks and then turned and locked into position. Kingsgate is the old name of Bow Lane which runs down beside St Mary-the-Bow Church to the site of a former postern gate in the city wall and a ford across the river. It commemorated the legend that William the Conqueror had forced his way down to the ford when fleeing from 'the wrath of St Cuthbert' after daring to interfere with Cuthbert's coffin.

THE DURHAM CARPET FACTORY.

THE DURHAM CARPET FACTORY in its heyday, a photograph of a drawing of 1888. Founded in 1815 by Gilbert Henderson, the factory expanded until it dominated Back Lane and Freeman's Place along the riverside and became the major city employer. In May 1903 Henderson's sold out to Crossley's of Halifax. Over three hundred jobs were lost, for Crossley's carried out a 'take-over and strip' policy and discontinued carpet production in Durham. A former Henderson employee, Hugh Mackay, rented some of the buildings and unwanted machinery and re-established the carpet industry in the city.

'MESSING ABOUT IN BOATS' has always been popular and fine weather usually brings people down to the river to enjoy themselves – as in this photograph taken on the day Alderman Luke opened the new Baths Bridge linking Gilesgate with the Elvets in 1962. The pleasant aspect contrasts strongly with the 'industrial' riverside scene above. (Mr J.O. Luke)

City Streets

THE MARKET PLACE, c. 1780, as drawn by Samuel Hieronymus Grimm. The many topographical drawings made by Grimm are in the British Library and are a useful source of information. Around 1900 J.G. Wilson, a solicitor of North Bailey, began copying Grimm's drawings of the city and later engaged a student to complete the series. This is one of the Wilson copies. It shows the old St Nicholas' Church, demolished in 1856, the Clayport Gate into the city and the fine houses on the east side of the Market Place (where Boots the Chemist now occupies the early 1930s building which was formerly owned by Doggarts).

ST NICHOLAS' CHURCH, the Market Place. Originally a Norman foundation and much altered in the following seven and a half centuries, this church was demolished in 1857 to make way for a new St Nicholas'; so this is a very early photograph indeed of Durham. It shows the east end as shortened and rebuilt in 1841, when most of the churchyard was also removed to make more space for the market stalls and the clutter of carts. (Mrs J. Stobbs)

NEPTUNE IN THE MARKET PLACE, 1863. Even after the 1848 Public Health Act the water supplied by the pant (or fountain) was still in demand and this was a popular place for 'a bit crack' (a chat). Neptune and the pant were under threat at this time; many people thought that they were too shabby for the new Town Hall, the 'New Markets', the re-built St Nicholas' and the Londonderry statue. They had their champions, however, and 'Neptune' wrote letters to the *Durham Chronicle* pleading his cause.

THE PANT IN THE MARKET PLACE, designed by E.R. Robson and erected in 1863. After much discussion the statue of Neptune was mounted on top. When first installed the pant had a bracket lamp at each corner, but these did not give adequate light and were replaced by the free-standing ones shown here. Water flowed into the troughs through stone animal heads, one of which survives in a Durham garden. (Mrs R.B. Macdonald)

THE 1902 PANT, THE MARKET PLACE. This photograph of a drawing by Robert J.S. Bertram of Newcastle upon Tyne shows the 'new' pant crowned with the old statue of Neptune against the backcloth of the Town Hall and St Nicholas' Church. Money for this pant was given by Miss Ellen Elizabeth Gibson, who also founded the university's Gibson Prize for Archaeology in memory of her brother William Sydney, a barrister and the author of a history of Tynemouth.

NEPTUNE ON TOP OF THE OLD PANT in the Market Place. As the 'New Markets' are in the background of this picture the photograph must have been taken after 1852, but no later than 16 September 1863, when this pant was demolished and the statue transferred to the new fountain. The teapot outside C.F. White's was later moved to Gilesgate and afterwards to James Fowler's in Claypath. It is now above Hammick's bookshop in Saddler Street. (Durham County Reference Library)

THE WEST SIDE OF DURHAM MARKET PLACE, c. 1922, with St Nicholas' looming in the mist behind. The clutter of motor bikes, cars and carts was already a serious problem by 1923, when the pant (no longer essential) was removed to make way for a much-needed police traffic-control box. Motor bikes were a popular form of transport, offering the less well-to-do a cheaper form of mechanical transport than the car. F.E. Coates, one of the architects of Durham's Shire Hall, was also a local pioneer of motor-bike design. The horse-drawn milk cart was a thing of the past by the end of the Second World War; milk measured from the churn for household deliveries vanished with the introduction of milk bottles and more stringent hygiene laws.

Below, left:
THE TOWN HALL, with the Guildhall to the left, c. 1966. The buildings, with three small shops beneath, were built by the Henry Smith Charity in 1852 and did not become part of the municipal buildings until 1915. The two windows over the shops are those of the Burlison Art Gallery housing works left to the city by Clement Burlison (1815–99). The gallery must surely have been the only one in the country at the time to be over a tobacconist's, a barber's and a fish-and-chip shop. In this more heritage-conscious age the shops serve as the city Tourist Information Centre.

DURHAM'S SATURDAY MARKET is a colourful affair nowadays with the stalls taking over the square; this was not the case during the inter-war years when cars and buses vied with market traders for space. Many stalls offered second-hand goods – an indication of hard times for the less well-off. The statue of the third Marquess of Londonderry presided over a drab scene then. The railings near the statue surround the steep steps down to the men's conveniences which monopolised much needed space; they were removed as part of the landscaping of the market place in 1975. The domed top of the policeman's box can be seen in the centre; this too has gone. The main banks are to be found in or near the market place. Barclays (the late-nineteenth-century building at the left next to the Evening Chronicle offices) may claim to be the oldest Durham bank as it bought out Backhouse and Company, the Quaker bankers who had premises on the site from the early nineteenth century. The imposing classical façade on the right is that of the National Provincial bank of 1876, designed by John Gibson.

THE MARKET PLACE, C. 1932; it is thought that the crowd is waiting for the results of a general election. Election results have been announced from the balcony of the Guildhall since 1673 when the city first had parliamentary representation. There has been a guildhall on this site since 1356; it was rebuilt by Bishop Tunstall in 1535 and again by Bishop Cosin in 1665. The present façade is the work of P.C. Hardwick in 1851 but within the building is basically Cosin's as renovated in 1752 by George Bowes who was twice mayor of the city and its MP. To the left of the Guildhall are the 'new' markets and to the right the Town Hall and offices. The whole block is remarkably restrained for a Victorian public building and in no way prepares the visitor for the delightful Mayor's Chamber and the sumptuous Town Hall with its hammer-beam roof.

WILLIAM SMITH'S DRAPERS' SHOP in the Market Place, c. 1930. Hepworth's occupied these premises for many years; more recently it was a branch of Next.

IN 1976 SILVER STREET AND ELVET BRIDGE were closed to traffic and so was much of the Market Place. A copy of this picture of the men who carried out the floorscaping scheme in the Market Place was included in a time capsule installed by the mayor, Councillor James Mackintosh, on Wednesday 14 July 1976. It is difficult to imagine the Market Place without Lord Londonderry's statue; it is the most prominent feature and a favourite meeting place. Yet when the council realized in 1861 just how big it was to be attempts were made to persuade the university to erect it on Palace Green instead. (Durham County Reference Library)

TRAFFIC-CONTROL BOX in the Market Place; the use of television cameras enabled one policeman to control the traffic of four approach roads. There is a 'Durham story' that there was only one particular policeman who was capable of dealing with the traffic at its worst, but that he was often given other duties as his forthright (and worse) comments outraged drivers; such as when he forcefully reprimanded a chauffeur for not following his instructions. Unfortunately the passenger was the chief constable and the order 'My office, ten-thirty!' was given. (Durham County Reference Library)

A LATE NINETEENTH-CENTURY SHOP-FRONT inserted into the eighteenth-century brickwork of Pullen Corner overlooking the Market Place masks a timber-framed building of around 1600, and an exuberant plasterwork ceiling which includes Neptune heads, Tudor roses and fleur-de-lys. In the 1890s it narrowly avoided demolition and was again threatened in the 1930s when Mr J. Bramwell and Dr W. Gibby successfully opposed the idea.

SADDLER STREET, C. 1912. This narrow thoroughfare has always been the main approach to the cathedral and many of the nineteenth- and early-twentieth-century façades along its ancient building line retain features belonging to earlier centuries. The Shakespeare Tavern owes its name to the Theatre Royal just behind it. The theatre was all but destroyed by fire in 1869 but it struggled on as a music hall for a time; it was then variously used as a tract and Bible depot, an exhibition hall, an art school, a piano salesroom and as an auctioneer's. It was demolished in 1974 to make way for student accommodation.

THE OLD WINE AND BEER VAULTS of the now vanished Golden Lion Hotel in Saddler Street. This illustration was used as a bill-heading around 1863. The vaults still exist under the former post office, erected on the site on 1898.

THE GAME AND POULTRY SHOP of T. Brown and Son in Silver Street presents a Dickensian ideal of Christmas cheer. (Durham University Library)

THE EARLS' CONFECTIONERY AND GAME BUSINESS is another example of the shop-keeping families which were the backbone of commercial activity in Durham until about 1960. Miss Connie Earl was the last member of the family to run the cake shop in Saddler Street. (Durham University Library)

FLESHERGATE (Fleshewergate), i.e., the butcher's area, looking towards the Market Place. The smell and the filth must have been appalling until the health reforms of the late nineteenth century. An early-nineteenth-century eye witness account mentions blood and piles of offal in the street, oxen bordering on madness being driven along to public slaughter in front of the shops and the great gratification derived by the boys and youths who watched 'this disgraceful and uncivilised practice'. The lamp post marks the junction of Fleshergate with Suter's Peth and Saddler Street. Excavations have shown that this area has been occupied from the tenth century. It had acquired the name of Saddlergate by the thirteenth century; by the fourteenth century the trade from which it had derived its name had largely moved away.

LAYING THE 'SETS' (i.e., the granite cobbles) at Magdelene Steps, c. 1897. This little stretch leading down to Elvet Bridge was the cobblers' quarter of the city and in order to widen the steps to their present width a tiny shop and cottage had to be demolished. The fine town-houses of Fleshergate can be seen in the background. Saddlergate was the leather-workers' area until the early fourteenth century. (Durham University Library)

ELVET WATERSIDE. A once pleasant riverside house, its outbuildings and adjoining cottages forlornly await development. The recent river terrace of the County Hotel extension and The Swan and Cygnets occupy this site now. As Elvet means 'swan island' the name of the public house was an appropriate choice.

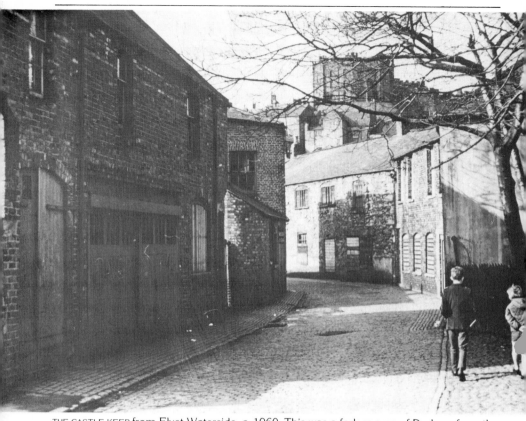

THE CASTLE KEEP from Elvet Waterside, c. 1960. This was a forlorn area of Durham from the early 1930s when there were the first whispers of a new road that would involve the demolition of property around here; so many of the buildings were 'left in limbo' but the cobbled street had a certain charm, especially on a sunlit afternoon such as the one the Kelly boys are enjoying here. Many people will remember Mr Peele's veterinary surgery which was here until the great changes of the 1960s. (Mr D.V. Kelly)

OLD ELVET, C. 1914. Water-troughs such as this one around the lamp post at the junction of the Elvets were essential in the age of the horse. It was installed in 1864 and removed when it became a traffic hazard. In the late nineteenth century the open area around the fountain was known as Appii Forum and Three Taverns by local schoolboys, who paid unauthorised visits to the three inns in the vicinity. Although a highly respectable street the far end of Old Elvet was frequented by prostitutes and illegal gamblers about whom there were many complaints.

THE DUNELM HOTEL, Old Elvet, c. 1925. John William Pattinson advertised that his Old Elvet Café could seat a hundred and that he was noted for pastries and cakes. The residential part of this temperance hotel ran above the café and its neighbour, John Gray's hardware and toy shop. (Durham County Reference Library)

OLD ELVET, looking east, 1952. It is rare now to see the most gracious street in the city at its best for it is usually cluttered with cars. The building beyond the white house was demolished and the University Chaplaincy built in its place in 1961. The little Grecian-style cast-iron balcony (partially hidden by a tree) is said to have been installed to give the early-nineteenth-century occupants of the house a grandstand view of the public executions outside the prison on the far side of Elvet Green. (Dr J.L. Crosby)

THE ASSIZE COURTS, OLD ELVET, completed in 1821. Begun in 1809 the building of the courts was a lengthy and costly business because of the poor workmanship and dishonest practices of the building contractors, which was aggravated by the negligence of one architect and the deviousness of a second. It was finally completed by Ignatius Bonomi, the County Architect, but not before it had cost the county a staggering £112,034 and put an extra $1\frac{1}{2}$d. on the rates.

COURT LANE has a dramatic view of the cathedral upon its rock. This lane was the boundary between the barony and the borough of Elvet and was called Raton Row (Ratonrawe) before the Assize Courts were built in 1814–21. Council houses, built in the 1930s, replaced some of the worst slums in Durham; those on the left remain but the ones in the centre distance were knocked down prior to the erection of new university buildings in 1962–6. (Mr D.V. Kelly)

NEW ELVET, C. 1912, looking down towards the junction with Old Elvet. Most of the houses in the foreground have gone. Those on the right, condemned as the 'rookeries' of Durham, were replaced by a neat mock-Tudor row of shops with an open space in front before the last war. Those on the left were demolished prior to the opening of Kingsgate Bridge and the building of Dunelm House. (Durham County Record Office)

A SMALL BUTCHERS' SHOP such as this was commonplace before the advent of the supermarket. Cattle were still being slaughtered behind these premises at the bottom of New Elvet in the late 1940s; they are now the Prontaprint offices. Although the notice says 'Estd: 1895', the name of Heslop occurs in the Butchers' Guild records of the seventeenth century when John Heslopp was ordered, 'that he forbear to sett John Ducke on worke in the trade of a butcher'. The monogram on the doorpost to the right is that of the Half Moon Inn, the fine front of which is still preserved. The notice 'Waterloo Hotel Annexe' is a reminder of the times when Durham was short of hotel accommodation and the now vanished Waterloo had to take over an extra building across the road.

DILAPIDATION SUCH AS THIS was typical among many of the older dwellings in the city around 1912, when coal-mining and trade generally suffered a mini-recession. Much property like this was swept away during the inter-war years as part of council clearance schemes. Two copies of this photograph have been found; one is labelled 'Hallgarth Street', the other 'New Elvet', so no firm identification can be offered.

THE TITHE BARN. This precious remnant of the Priory Hallgarth Farm is tucked away down a lane off Hallgarth Street. It now serves as a prison officers' club. The ground floor is stone built; the upper floor is partly of vertically studded timber and partly brick. Nearby there are out-buildings and a byre also belonging to the Priory Farm. Elvet Hall or Hallgarth belonged to the monastery until the Dissolution; it was sometimes used as a guest-house for important visitors. A document of 1371 refers to sumptuous bed-covers adorned with lilies, roses, butterflies, eagles and leopards.

COLLY RIPPON'S LANE, a lost and forgotten fragment of old Durham in the Margery Lane–Neville's Cross area. (Durham University Library)

GOING HOME FROM MARKET. It is difficult to believe that this nineteenth-century drawing of the toll-house and gate beside the stump of the cross commemorating the victory over the Scots in 1346 is now one of the busiest areas in Durham – the busy crossroads where the A690 intersects the A167 (the Great North Road) and where a new bypass is under consideration.

THE FIRE AT MACKAY'S ruined most of the fine stone buildings erected in the 1840s and accelerated the factory's move to Dragonville on the city outskirts. It also left a planning problem: what should happen to this site so close to the heart of the cathedral city? An acceptable answer has yet to be found; whatever happens, the cathedral and castle skyline must not be challenged nor must too much extra traffic flow be generated to exacerbate the already severe problem of traffic and car-parking. (Mr D.V. Kelly)

JAMES FOWLER'S GROCERY SHOP closed and awaiting demolition. The building had been a substantial three-storey house, but had been reduced in size when the top floor became dilapidated. Fowler's were the custodians of the famous teapot for many years. The Fowler family was well known in the city. James Fowler had established the Claypath shop by 1853; three members of the family have served the city as mayor. Alderman James Fowler was mayor five times (1872, 1881–4 and 1886) and was given the honorary freedom of the city in 1885. (Mr D.V. Kelly)

PARADISE LANE or Rashell's Lane. This cobbled lane ran from the northeast corner of the Market Place down towards the ford near Elvet bridge just outside the line of the medieval city wall. The name 'Paradise' seems inept but it was sometimes given to pathways similiarly excluded from a walled town and this particular lane formerly deserved its name for it ran alongside lovely Paradise Gardens and house. There was still an old-style tinsmith working in the lane around 1960; there was also an unofficial bookie who made it his patch and who would just 'melt away' whenever a stranger or policeman appeared. The lane was virtually obliterated by the building works of the mid-1960s. (Mr D.V. Kelly)

THE BIG JUG HOTEL, CLAYPATH, 'an entirely free house', c. 1928, when John W. Thompson was the publican. The pub and its distinctive sign function still. It is one of the relatively few public houses surviving in a street which less than eighty years ago was described as being awash with inns and taverns.

THE BURTON HOTEL, 215 Gilesgate, c. 1897, when it was kept by G.W.C. Burnett who followed Henry Barnes as publican. Its name was changed to the Baths Bridge. It had ceased to be a public house by 1925.

A SNOW SCENE, May 1917, taken from Ravensworth Terrace. The group of houses on the extreme right were demolished to make way for the new Leazes Road; above them Gilesgate bank can be seen. The two houses on the upper left (Nos 210 and 209), and those beyond the gap, remain; the gap was the site of The Nagg's Head. In 1698 that fearless traveller Celia Fiennes (an ancestor of Rannulf) found it difficult to find an inn free of the 'randan' of parliamentary elections until, 'I happen'd to get into a quiet, good inn, and good accommodation, two maiden sisters and brother kept it, at the Nagg's Head'. A house was built on the site in the 1930s by the Holiday family who built the Palladium Cinema in Claypath. (Mrs J. Stobbs)

NOW VANISHED BUILDINGS in lower Gilesgate seen here before the Second World War, probably around 1930. This pantiled row of boarded-up shops was said to contain early seventeenth-century features. They have since been replaced by a row of cottages set back a little from the earlier building line.

MISS H. WHITE AND MRS E. VASEY, the proprietors of a grocery shop and post office at 30 Gilesgate, c. 1892. The shop was in lower Gilesgate just before Moody's Buildings; the row of houses was demolished in the inter-war years and a pair of semi-detached houses built on part of the site. These were also demolished, to make way for the new road and roundabout. (Durham University Library)

ST GILES' CHURCH, pre-1914, looking up the path from the raised pavement of Gilesgate to the early Norman north wall with its three original windows and to the porch added in 1873–6. The railings and the formal flower beds have gone, as have the houses on the left, which were replaced by council houses in the mid-1960s in a neo-Georgian style – a praiseworthy attempt to build the new in harmony with the old. (Mrs J. Stobbs)

THE INTERIOR OF ST GILES' CHURCH showing the north wall with one of its three remaining Norman windows; this is all that remains of the original hospital chapel founded in 1112 by Bishop Flambard. The hospital was a guest-house for pilgrims to the shrine of St Cuthbert and was very conveniently placed for pilgrims travelling on the main road from Bishop and Monk Wearmouth and Houghton-le-Spring. (Durham University Library)

THE WHITE BEAR INN at Kepier was originally the residence of the Tempest family, who in turn had acquired the Kepier estate thirty years after the suppression of the medieval hospital. The inn was still functioning in 1854 when Thomas Gibson was the innkeeper, though it had closed by 1893, when it was occupied by Thomas Harper, and still referred to as Kepier Inn. Only the stone loggia of the Tempest house remains; its broad balustered oak staircase, great hall and the remains of once splendidly carved panelling, observed by a local historian in 1892, have gone. It is said that the staircase and panelling were removed in the 1920s to a house in South Shields. (Durham University Library)

KEPIER GATEWAY, formerly the gatehouse of St Giles' Hospital, Kepier. The original hospital was founded in Gilesgate and was rebuilt on the pleasant riverside site at Kepier c. 1180. This fourteenth-century gatehouse was built by Bishop de Bury. It is an impressive relic of an important foundation where Edward I stayed on his way to fight the Scots in 1298 and where Queen Isabella stayed in 1310. Although run down when suppressed in 1545 it had been well endowed with tithes and estates, including an iron mine and a dairy farm in Weardale.

A VIEW OF SILVER STREET, C. 1920, before shops such as Woolworth's and Marks and Spencer were built and at a time when trade was depressed. In the distance are houses in South Street.

SILVER STREET, C. 1933. The unsuitability of this cobbled street for motor vehicles is clearly shown at this, its narrowest point – only 11 ft wide. Beyond the bus are the tripartite windows of the former Castle Hotel. The building next to it is, and remains, Dunn's the outfitters; the pathway alongside it leads to 'broken walls' and to Palace Green. There was a vennel (or alley) between the draper's and Gillow's (on the left) which linked up with Moatside Lane; it vanished around 1960. The virtual rebuilding of Gillow's in 1989/90 revealed the line of the old vennel and also timber-framing indicating the building's ancient history.

SILVER STREET, C. 1935. Still retaining its medieval width, Silver Street was ill-equipped to deal with modern traffic and from 1922 traffic was regulated by an alternate one-way system; this caused increasing congestion during the years after the war, which the installation of television cameras helped to alleviate. It is now kept free of traffic for the greater part of each day. The buildings at top right were demolished to make way for Marks and Spencer's.

THE ROSE AND CROWN HOTEL, Silver Street, now the site of Woolworths. The Rose and Crown stood here when Charles I visited Durham; tradition says that he was presented with a piece of silver by the citizens here. The hotel boasts a 'motor garage' where earlier it had advertised extensive stabling. Next door is Harry Battensby's Albion House, Nos 1 and 2, where clothing of every description was sold. The two brothers began the business around 1872 and it remained a family firm for about sixty years. Tucked away behind Battensby's shop was Albion Court which was home for five or six families. Marks and Spencer continue the tradition of the retail clothes trade on the site but there is no modern equivalent of Albion Court.

SILVER STREET. Herman Strathman, shoemaker, had established his shop at No. 6 by 1872, premises which he shared initially with J.G. Mohun, a currier. His advertisements are markedly different from the style of today's 'admen': 'H.S. in returning thanks to his numerous Customers and Public in general, begs to inform them that he has always on hand a large stock of HOME-MADE BOOTS & SHOES, and all orders will receive prompt attention on reasonable terms.' Today Silver Street is wholly commercial; there are no private residents; yet in the 1870s most shopkeepers lived 'over the shop' and there were other occupants including miners and labourers. There was a Strathman's shoe shop in Silver Street until the early 1960s and a second shop in North Road from around 1924.

A LOST VIEW. Major demolition in Silver Street prior to the extension of Marks and Spencer produced this unusual view of the west side of Silver Street. On the extreme right is the curving wall of Moatside Lane, which runs from the lower part of the street to Saddler Street. It is an ancient path skirting the castle walls. (Durham City Planning Office)

DURHAM, FROM WEAR BRIDGE.

FRAMWELLGATE BRIDGE and the foot of Silver Street, c. 1877, a surprisingly rural scene for a city centre. John Balmborough's 'Ainsley's original mustard manufactory' (at the left) was one of three power-driven mustard mills in the city; the others were William Ainsley's in Saddler Street (now Hammick's books) and in Waddington Street; and Simpson and Willan in Gilesgate. A Mrs Clements of Durham is said to have invented mustard in 1720. It quickly became popular under the patronage of George II who (or so the legend goes) had a fondness for the lady as well as for her invention. Her secret recipe passed to the Ainsley's; and the last factory sold out to Colman's in c. 1897.

ALBERT HOUSE, SILVER STREET, for over a century George Greenwell and Sons' high-class grocery store, whose respected name is still remembered by Mr Sydney Davison's shop 'Greenwells in Archibalds' in North Road. F. Greenwell had a shop in the Market Place which became Hutchinson and Greenwell and was advertised as being established in 1745. However, George Greenwell set up on his own at 2 Silver Street in 1850 when No. 33, Albert House, was a public house of the same name kept by William Marshall and named in honour of Prince Albert. Greenwell's stayed at No. 33 from c. 1860 and when they expanded into a former chapel at the rear of the premises they installed a steam coffee-grinding machine. A café, opened upstairs before the Second World War, was re-opened a few years after the war ended. Greenwell's closed down in 1982 after the death of Mr George Greenwell. (Durham University Library)

THE PLACING OF THE TELEVISION CAMERAS had to be very accurate if they were going to relay the required information to the screen in the policeman's traffic-control box in the Market Place. These technicians are trying out positions for the camera overlooking Framwellgate Bridge in January 1950. (Durham County Reference Library)

THE VIEW FROM THE CASTLE after the new County Library (on lower left with flat roof) was built in 1961, but before the demolition works which preceded the building of the Milburngate shopping precinct. The commanding position of the castle over Framwellgate Bridge and the approach to the city is clearly shown. The bridge formerly carried all the traffic from the west into the city and was guarded by a gateway in medieval times. It was pedestrianized in 1976.

Below, left:
WOOLWORTH'S, SILVER STREET, c. 1938. Decorated for Christmas and nothing over 6 d.; there were several things obtainable for less – a bar of chocolate for 1 d.; Christmas decorations, two for 1½ d.; and a reel of cotton for 2 d. A camera could be bought for 5 s., but the promise 'Nothing in these stores over 6 d.' was kept: the various parts of the camera were individually priced at 6 d., or less; the snag was that you had to buy all the parts at one and the same time. (Durham University Library)

THE FOOT OF SOUTH STREET, c. 1960. The Dunelm Court housing development replaced the two large buildings in 1975. These were the Johnston Technical School, founded with money bequeathed by James Finlay Weir Johnston, the first Reader in Chemistry and Mineralogy at the university and a prolific writer. The lower building was erected in 1899 and the second stage in 1906. The present Johnston Comprehensive School commemorates the old school and its founder.

THE WEST SIDE of lower South Street, c. 1960. South Street offers an incomparable view of the western façade of the cathedral and is a much sought after residential location. The house with the steps was formerly the home of Mr and Mrs B. Colgrave. Bertram Colgrave was Reader in Anglo-Saxon at the university and editor of two near-contemporary 'Lives' of St Cuthbert.

GRAPE LANE, OFF CROSSGATE, survives only in name. The cobbled lane and old houses, some with pantile roofs, had great charm but unfortunately were allowed to decay and were replaced by a row of trim modern houses.

THE OLD FRAMWELLGATE PETH, c. 1900. Peth is a northern word for hill; Framwellgate Peth, leading up to Aykley Heads, was for centuries the main road out of Durham to Newcastle and the north. In the seventeenth century Framwellgate was home to many prosperous brewers, dyers and tanners, but by late Victorian times their substantial houses had become slum tenements and by the mid-1930s the buildings were condemned. Efforts to save and restore them failed. The council housing built to replace the tenements was demolished in the large scale developments of the mid-1960s.

A WAREHOUSE, c. 1920, with a cart from the Lambton and Hett Colliery Company; it was in the Framwellgate waterside area and no longer exists.

BLAGDON'S LEATHER WORKS on Framwellgate waterside was a prominent landmark for over a century until its demolition in the sweeping changes of the mid-1960s. George Blagdon's business was already well established by 1854 in old premises next door to this major late nineteenth-century extension. By 1874 the family no longer 'lived over the shop' but had moved to a new villa in Redhills and later to Pelaw Terrace – both well away from the noxious fumes associated with their trade. A third George Blagdon specialized in horse trappings and harnesses, and had a shop in Claypath. (Mr D.V. Kelly).

NORTH ROAD at night, c. 1910. This carefully touched-up photograph gives North Road a glamour it certainly did not possess by day. Critics condemned North Road as a street more suited to a mining village than to a cathedral city. But North Road was a shopping street for miners, as was Silver Street, the Market Place and Claypath. Miners and their families poured into Durham every Saturday for shopping and when cheap day-returns on the railway tempted the miners to Newcastle and Darlington the city traders were badly hit.

NORTH ROAD, with the castle in the background. This was taken before the changes of the mid-1960s: traffic is still using Framwellgate Bridge, and the King William IV is still on the corner on the left, with Oliver's fish and game shop just beyond at the beginning of Milburngate. The building on the right-hand corner of the bridge is still standing. The entrance to Reform Place (1832) may be seen on the near left; it still has the original carved name plate on the wall. Beyond Reform Place is Lindsley's Buildings, named after a former owner, Richard Lindsley, who in the last thirty years or so of the nineteenth century was both horse dealer and china and glass dealer.

A DESERTED NORTH ROAD, C. 1925. Porter's the grocer's is at the corner of Neville Street. This block of property was demolished when the electricity showrooms were built in the early 1960s. Porter's was a well-known trader in the city for nearly a century. John Porter had a shop in lower Gilesgate by 1872 and Porter's remained there until the building was demolished prior to the construction of the relief road in about 1962. They also had a shop on Elvet Bridge. Joseph Moffat Lynch was a name well known to shoppers during the inter-war years and after. He had a block of four shops in North Road selling clothes, hardware, material, china and glass. He was mayor in 1927. Beyond Lynch's shop are the well-built offices of the Durham Water Company, founded in 1866. The building was erected soon after the company amalgamated with the Weardale and Shildon District waterworks. By 1893 the company had built several service reservoirs and the great reservoir at Tunstall, Wolsingham, which has a capacity of 520,000,000 gallons and has enhanced the natural beauty of that area.

THE IRON AND GLASS ARCADES of the bus station in North Road stood in what had been the grounds of a house built in 1842 for Mr Robson, whose corn mill was close by. The house is now the bus company's office, the mill has gone, and the stream which served it is confined in an underground culvert. The bus station remains, but this arcading was dismantled about fifteen years ago, taken to Beamish Museum and stored for possible re-use. (Mr D.V. Kelly)

FOUNTAINS OFFERING 'PURE WATER' to the general public were often installed by local benefactors in the nineteenth century. This Durham example, in 'French Gothic' style, was fed by water from Flass Vale and was erected by public subscription in 1868. Displaced by demolition preparatory to the major roadworks of the mid-1960s, it was removed to another part of the railway viaduct at the top of North Road.

HOUSES CLUSTERED UNDER THE RAILWAY VIADUCT. The building of the railway and the station to the north-west side of the city resulted in the building of several terraces of working-class homes such as these in New Street. The draining of the land enabled houses to be built and relatively cheap fares and proximity to the station meant that people could commute to their work.

ALTERATIONS IN NORTH ROAD, c. 1935. At the right is the former Miners' Hall. When it was built the Miners' Union had 60,000 members; but by 1914 that number had more than doubled and the miners had moved to the grander buildings in Redhills Lane. The old hall's ground floor was used for shops and the upstairs for public meetings. In the late 1920s the shops next to the hall were demolished and the Miners' Hall was transformed by the Crown Billiards Company into the Regal Cinema and Ballroom with billiards and pool tables, but only after many expensive delays due to flooding on the site.

TENTER TERRACE: the name of this little row of houses is a reminder of the woollen cloth industry so important in eighteenth-century Durham. The tenter was the machine for stretching cloth to set or dry, or the person in charge of the process. The area was well provided with the streams and springs needed for the cloth industry. *The Lion in Winter*, advertised on the hoarding, was issued in 1968. The Essoldo Cinema later changed its name to the Classic; the only survivor of the five cinemas formerly in the city, it was closed down on 28 June 1990. (Mr D.V. Kelly)

DURHAM FROM WHARTON PARK. Wharton Park was part of the estate of William Lloyd Wharton of Aykley Heads; he often opened this part of his estate to the general public on high days and holidays. In 1915 his daughter, Mrs Darwin, gave the park to the people of Durham. The park has magnificent views over the city and of the eleven great arches of the viaduct, each 100 ft high. Tremendous expense and back-aching labour were required to build the viaduct, not only on account of its size but because it was built on marshy ground that included the peat bogs of Chilton pool. Great oak trunks were sunk about 50 ft down to give stability to the structure.

THE LYCHGATE leading to St Bede's Cemetery, Redhills. This delightfully rural scene is barely half a mile from the bus and railway stations and the bustle of North Road. The cemetery chapel was erected in 1867; a piscina and a window from the thirteenth-century private chapel of the ancient Harbour House Farm near Chester-le-Street were reused in it. It was deconsecrated about twenty years ago and is now a house. (Mr D.V. Kelly)

THE INTERIOR of the church of St Margaret of Antioch, Crossgate. This church, of Norman origin, was built as a chapel of ease to St Oswald's. The slim pillars of the graceful north arcade are late Norman. The stained-glass window used to be at the east end until replaced by the Good Samaritan window in memory of the Revd P.S. Wilkinson of Mount Oswald. Sir John Duck, who was Mayor of Durham in 1680, is buried in the nave. His rags-to-riches career, his charitable works and high office have caused him to be called Durham's Dick Whittington. He owned no cat however, but owed his good fortune to a raven who dropped a gold coin at his feet.

ALLERGATE (originally Alvertongate), one of the city's medieval streets and part of the old borough (Crossgate). By the end of the fifteenth century most of Allergate belonged to the monastery and details survive of the rents received by the sacrist and almoner. There was a stone-built house in Allergate as early as 1296 belonging to Thomas Blagriseit, but this boarded-up building is of much later time. It was the Infirmary for the Sick and Lame Poor erected in 1793 by public subscription on land given by Thomas Wilkinson of Coxhoe. It arose from the dispensary in Saddler Street run by Dr Salkeld and was replaced by a new hospital at the top of North Road in 1854. (Durham University Library)

People and Places

MR MICHAEL MAWSON OF GILESGATE, the father of Joseph and the grandfather of Joseph Landt Mawson, enjoying a quiet smoke on his clay pipe in his garden, c. 1910. Clay pipes were widely used until the 1930s; up to the First World War there were at least four pipe makers in the city. They were still used by older men in the late 1940s. In cold weather some smokers would shorten the stem of their pipe so that the bowl was nearly under their nose – they claimed it kept them warm. (Mrs J. Stobbs – his great granddaughter)

A VICTORIAN ANGLER: Mr William Henderson (c. 1812–72). Part-owner with his brother John of the carpet factory, a councillor from 1835, mayor of the city in 1849, a leading instigator of local public health reform and the building of the new Town Hall (his monogram is on the hall's chimney-piece) and author of a work on northern folklore, William's great hobby was trout fishing. His *Notes and Reminiscences of an Angler* indicate that his passion began as soon as he had been 'breeched' and continued unabated throughout his life.

A SALVATION ARMY family group photographed by the J.R. Edis studio which was *the* photographic studio in the city for about sixty years. John Edis and his daughter Daisy were widely known in church and university circles. Daisy Edis popping in and out of the black cloth over her camera was a familiar sight in the colleges during the summer term's round of 'year' and team photographs. The carved chair in which the commissioner is seated was part of the Edis 'props'. Fortunately many of the Edis photographs survive, though many subjects cannot be identified, including this group, whose sensitive faces make us want to know more about them. (Durham University Library)

THE DURHAM CONTINGENT for the review by the king in Windsor Great Park in 1911. Joseph L. Mawson (centre front) is rehearsing with his colleagues of the University Corps in the castle courtyard. (Mrs J. Stobbs)

ENEMY TARGETS for the gymkhana of 1916. Kaiser Bill, the Sultan of Turkey, Hindenberg, the Crown Prince and von Spee replaced the traditional targets for the coconut shy in a wartime fund-raising effort. (Mrs J. Stobbs)

AN ENEMY ZEPPELIN over Durham, December 1916. J.L. Mawson reacted quickly to record this unexpected visitor; his next shot showed the Zeppelin bursting into flames over West Hartlepool and was published in a local newspaper. (Mrs J. Stobbs)

THE DECLARATION OF PEACE in 1918 was formally announced from the balcony of the Guildhall by the mayor, George Henderson Proctor; a scene that had its counterpart in towns up and down the country. The end of one of the most crippling wars ever fought was greeted with an almost hysterical relief, but the peace did not bring about 'a land fit for heroes'.

MEMBERS OF THE BRITISH LEGION assembling in the Market Place for their procession up to the cathedral for the Remembrance Day Service in November 1921. Until the outbreak of the Second World War in 1939 a two-minute silence was observed throughout the country at the eleventh hour of the eleventh day of the eleventh month every year to commemorate the signing of the Armistice. (Durham County Reference Library)

'LEST WE FORGET' – the first Poppy Day, 1921. The British Legion Fund was founded by Earl Haig to give help to the families of men killed in the First World War and to the disabled and unemployed ex-service men and women. The Legion still works for the survivors of two world wars. The first Poppy Day collectors in Durham are on the steps of the Town Hall with the mayor, Councillor William Smith. (Mrs J. Stobbs)

A MILITARY DINNER in the impressive setting of the Town Hall for officers of the Durham Light Infantry, possibly when Alderman Matthew Fowler was mayor, c. 1890.

Below, left:
'LIDDELL FOR EVER', 'Poll Plumpers for Liddell', and 'Queen and Constitution' declare the banners as the populace celebrates the election of Liddell. Henry Liddell, together with Hedworth Lambton, was elected to parliament for the northern division in 1837 and 1841. This painting is thought to depict the 1837 election, when 'Chairing the Member' around the town was 'the usual custom', but by 1852 it was described as 'nearly obsolete'; the chair was kept in the Guildhall. A 'poll plumper' was an elector who, having the right to vote for two candidates, opts to support only one. The Market Place is recorded before the major changes of the next twenty years. The Guildhall (on the left) still has Bishop Cosin's façade of 1665, while the jettied former town-house, forfeited by the Nevilles in 1569, still stands, as does the ancient St Nicholas' Church and the piazza for stall-holders in front of the church.

JUDGES AT A FLOWER AND VEGETABLE SHOW in Durham Town Hall, c. 1920. The popularity of such shows waned as the age of television took hold but the tradition persisted and is enjoying a revival in the present 'green' atmosphere and the urban nostalgia for the 'good life'. (Durham County Reference Library)

EDWARDIAN ELEGANCE in the Town Hall. Fine rugs and bowls of flowers tastefully arranged on small tables suggest a special occasion. Such occasions have been commonplace in this Town Hall and all the others up and down the country; this particular arrangement is thought to have been for the mayoress's 'At Home'; an annual event still held by the Mayoresses of Durham including the present Mayoress, Mrs Joan Crooks.

THE DURHAM LIGHT INFANTRY marching through the Market Place in May 1974; the mayor (Councillor John James Ramshaw, BEM), escorted by his bodyguard, took the salute. This was the beginning of the first mayoralty of the 'new' city of Durham created by the reorganization of local government. (Durham County Reference Library)

THE STATUE OF THE 3RD MARQUESS OF LONDONDERRY (1778–1854) in the Market Place. Londonderry inherited his title and estates following the death of his half-brother, Lord Castlereagh; he acquired even greater wealth by his marriage to Frances Anne Vane-Tempest, who managed the vast family estates after his death efficiently and imperiously and who initiated this statue, which was erected in 1861. In 1953 the statue was removed for restoration and a few months later, on a quiet Sunday morning, it was lifted back on to its plinth by these cranes belonging to a hire firm with the somewhat inappropiate name of Tremble.

THE DURHAM LIGHT INFANTRY – the Old Faithfuls – had the freedom of the city from 1944. Their contribution in war and peace was often recognized by the city. Here the last Mayor of the old city of Durham, Councillor Gordon McIntyre is inspecting a guard of honour from the DLI on 22 March 1974. On 1 April the reorganization of local government became effective and the following day Councillor J.J. Ramshaw assumed office as chairman of the new Durham District Council. (Durham County Reference Library)

Below, right:
THE COMPLETION OF THE FLOORSCAPING SCHEME in the Market Place in 1976 was commemorated by the unveiling of the indicator plate by the mayor, Councillor James Mackintosh, and his wife. (Durham County Reference Library)

THE LIFE-SIZE STATUE of the Polish dwarf, Count Joseph Borulawski, who lived in the city from 1822 until his death in 1837. The count's statue, together with his violin, a suit of clothes and one of his little wicker-chairs are displayed in the Town Hall. The count seems to have been a very popular figure in local circles and some households had suitable chairs made for when they entertained him. (Two were given to the city but only one survives.) Most visitors are intrigued by the count's small stature and his story; here Councillor Gordon McIntyre is talking about the count to a group of Norwegian students in 1974. See p. 121. (Durham County Reference Library)

AN UNUSUAL VIEW of the statue of the Marquess of Londonderry. John Atkinson and Wilf Belshaw carried out minor repairs in 1975 to the statue, which, at the time of its unveiling in 1861, was described as 'one of the largest works of art in the world'. It was designed by an Italian sculptor, Rafaele Monti, and was constructed by the galvano-plastic, or electro-plating, process. This was the first use on such a grand scale of a fairly new process and was welcomed as a major technological breakthrough. Monti promised to design a pant worthy of his equestrian statue but he did not keep his word. (Durham County Reference Library)

THE LAST MEETING of the Durham Rural Urban Council; a commemorative photograph taken on 29 March 1974. Mr James Ramshaw, the chairman, is wearing his chain of office. In the second row, second from the right, is Councillor Harry Barker, headmaster of Framwellgate Moor School. (Durham County Reference Library)

DURHAM AUTOMOBILE CLUB: presentation of awards on 28 November 1962, including one to a long-standing member, Mr J.L. Mawson. On the right the Mayor and Mayoress, Councillor and Mrs Raymond Appleby of Southlands, Gilesgate, can be seen. Belmont-born Mr Appleby was a master butcher; in addition to many civic duties he and his wife did a lot of work for many local charities including Cancer Research. (Mrs J. Stobbs)

THE MAYOR OF DURHAM, Councillor Robert Clewes, unveiling the restored statue of Neptune in the Town Hall in 1986. Presented to the city by George Bowes, an ancestor of the Queen Mother, the statue adorned three successive pants in the Market Place from 1727 until 1923 when it was banished to Wharton Park. In 1978 it was struck by lightning. The City of Durham Trust initiated a fund for its restoration which was carried out by Andrew Naylor of Telford. See pp. 50, 51, 106. (The City of Durham Trust)

PUPILS FROM BEAR PARK SCHOOL at the celebration to mark the restoration of Neptune in 1986. They performed a song about Neptune, written and composed by their teacher, Miss Clare Martin, who is at the piano. (City of Durham Trust)

THE MAYOR OF 1966/7 with her council, chaplain, bodyguard, mace-bearer and sword-bearer. Well known local personalities include: the Dean of Durham, the Revd J.H.S. Wild, Aldermen H. Cecil Ferens, Jack Shepherd and Mrs. E. Blyth (in the front row). In the second row: Norman Richardson OBE and Norman Sarsfield, formerly prominent in international swimming circles. Raymond Appleby and J.O. Luke are in the third row and John Williamson is in the fourth. Colin Beswick is near the back. All have been mayors or aldermen of the city.

AN ANNUAL CIVIC SERVICE is held each year in the cathedral. This photograph is of the procession to the 1966 service; it was led by the mayor, Mrs M.A. Thornhill and the town clerk and recorder, Mr David Martin-Jones. Alderman Mrs Evelyn Blyth is the only other woman in the procession. In 1954 she was Durham's second lady Mayor; Mrs Hannah Rushford was the first in 1950 and Mrs Thornhill the third. Behind Mrs Blyth is another former mayor, Mr Norman Richardson (1963); both have received the rare privilege of the honorary freedom of the city. Medallions worn by members in the procession indicate that they have been mayors. (Mrs M.A. Thornhill)

TWENTY-SIX PIECES OF FINE SILVER belonging to the Freemen's Guilds were formally presented to the city in July 1966 by the modern wardens of the ancient tradesmen's guilds. Left to right are: D. Blagdon (Curriers'), J. Nelson (Butchers'), L.E. Anderson (chairman of the wardens), H. Elliot, A.C. Clark (Masons'), and J.H. Vest (Tailors' and Drapers'). Most of the silver was made in the sixteenth and seventeenth centuries and carry the now rare Newcastle upon Tyne assay mark. The heaviest piece (53 oz) was given to the Butchers' Guild in 1782 by Hugh Percy, the son of the Duke of Northumberland. (Mrs M.A. Thornhill)

'TOWN AND GOWN' join together to welcome a new bishop on the occasion of his first service in the cathedral. This is the procession of 1966 when the Bishop of Durham, the Rt Revd Ian Ramsay was escorted from the castle, where he had been robed, to the cathedral. In the front row (left to right) are: Dr S. Holgate, Pro-Vice-Chancellor and Principal of Grey College and the Revd H. Absalom of St Hild's. In the second row are: Dr Derman Christopherson, Vice-Chancellor; the Earl of Scarborough, Chancellor of the University; the mayor, Mrs M. Thornhill; and the town clerk, Mr Martin-Jones. (Mrs M.A. Thornhill)

THE MAYOR'S BODYGUARD, SWORD-BEARER AND SERGEANT-AT-MACE (Mr J. Harrison) escorting the mayor to the Remembrance Day service in the cathedral, 1966. The origin of the captain and twelve men of the bodyguard may be traced back to the thirteenth century when they protected the warden of the city. Their task of guarding the mayor dates from 1602 when the first mayor was appointed. Durham is the only city other than London to have a mayoral bodyguard. Neither the bodyguard nor the bearer of the civic sword (here Mr H. Ingram) are needed today, though they greatly enhance special occasions. The silver mace is still significant for it symbolizes the mayor's authority and carries the names of the four bishops who granted charters to the city. (Mrs M.A. Thornhill)

REVD GEORGE MARCHANT, Vicar of St Nicholas', with some of his parishioners, watching the mayor cut the first sod for the church youth centre on the Sands in March 1967. Revd Marchant was a lively and caring minister whose services were very popular with university students. He later became Archdeacon of Auckland and was followed at St Nicholas' by Dr George Carey, later Bishop of Bath and Wells, and now Archbishop of Canterbury designate. (Mrs M.A. Thornhill)

WHEN EDWARD SHORT, then Postmaster General, was entertained at the jubilee dinner of the Post Office Savings Certificate Division in 1966, his visit to the city was a homecoming for him and C.F. Grey, MP (at the left), for both were from County Durham and Mr Short had been a student at Bede College. (Mrs M.A. Thornhill)

SINCE THE DAYS of pilgrimages to St Cuthbert's shrine the city has attracted visitors and, although modern pilgrims come for different reasons, the cathedral and the Market Place are always part of their itinerary. Here the mayor, Mrs M.A. Thornhill, and two former mayoresses, Mrs McIntyre and Mrs Williamson, are entertaining a group of overseas students together with their host Professor Scott (at the front). (Mrs M.A. Thornhill)

THE SPEAKER OF THE HOUSE OF COMMONS, Dr H.K. King at St Aidan's College in June 1966 when he opened the new college building designed by Sir Basil Spence, the architect of Coventry Cathedral. Dr King was awarded an honorary doctorate in law at a special congregation held in the college. Leading the procession is Sir James Duff, then Lord Lieutenant of the county. Previously Sir James had been Vice-Chancellor of the University; his successor in that post was Dr D.G. Christopherson, seen here walking behind Dr King. Dr Christopherson later became Master of Magdelene College, Cambridge, and was knighted. (Mrs M.A. Thornhill)

A NEWLY ELECTED MAYOR and his mayoress leaving the Town Hall: Councillor John Williamson and his wife in May 1967. Mr and Mrs Williamson kept a children's outfitters on Framwellgate Bridge; the premises have drastically altered and are now occupied by Pizzaland. On Mayor-Making Day the bodyguard elect their captain. (Mrs M.A. Thornhill)

THE MARKET PLACE *en fête* for the coronation of George V and Queen Mary in 1911. (Durham County Reference Library)

A PRESENTATION at Durham railway station in 1925. A solitary policeman guards justices, local dignitaries and a crowd of onlookers watching the chairman, Sir Walter Plummer, and Mr E.F. Wilkinson being presented to King George V and Queen Mary.

THE VISIT OF THE PRINCESS ROYAL (the daughter of King George V and later Countess of Harewood). The princess is seen leaving the Town Hall escorted by the mayor. The 'Ladies Toilet, open weekdays' notice looms overhead, somewhat *de trop* given the conventions of the day, but worse still, directly in HRH's line of vision are the men's public conveniences, erected in 1901. Admittedly they were underground but they were clearly advertised by the ornamental iron railings around the entrance and the notice upon them. Banks of potted plants, skilfully placed, ensured that potential embarassment to the royal visitor was avoided. The princess' main duty on her visit was to open a hospital wing.

THE QUEEN meeting civic dignitaries in 1974, attended by the mayor, Councillor Gordon McIntyre. She is shaking hands with a former mayor; Alderman J.O. Luke and then Councillor N. Richardson wait their turn to be introduced to Her Majesty. (Mr J.O. Luke)

THE MAYOR IN FULL REGALIA seated in the mayor's chair, which carries the city crest. The cockade on the official hat indicates the close connection with the bishops; the fur-trimmed robe, lace jabot, white gloves and the chain of office are all the outward symbols of the authority of the city's chief citizen, whose lineage goes back to 1602, when Bishop Tobias Matthew granted the Charter of Incorporation (confirmed by James I in 1605) allowing the burgesses to elect a mayor, alderman and commonalty. (Mrs M.A. Thornhill)

POLICEMEN escorting HM judges from the castle to the Assize Courts at the head of Elvet in 1901. The coachman, two flunkies and footmen are dressed in eighteenth-century style livery. Charles Hill's family grocery business occupied a prominent position on Elvet Bridge; it had been founded around 1850 by Benjamin Hill junior, and Hill and Sons were still in business in the late twenties. E. Brookes, the greengrocer's next door, had two other shops in the city and the family had nurseries at Shincliffe to supply the shops with fresh produce.

HM JUDGES processing into the cathedral for the 'Assize Sunday' service which is held when the judges are in residence (c. 1965). When the castle was given to the university as its founding college it was stipulated that a suite of rooms was to be reserved for the judges when the assizes were being held.

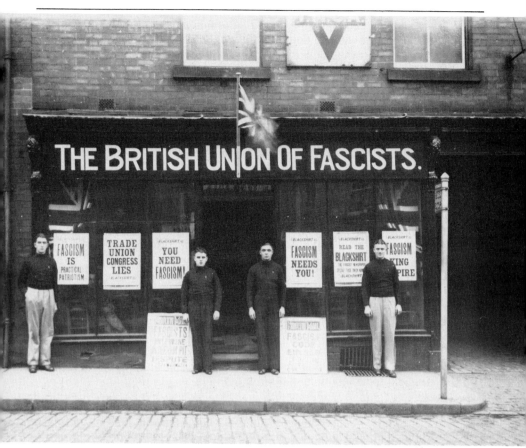

THE BRITISH UNION OF FASCISTS' office in Claypath, c. 1936. A swing to extreme authoritarian right-wing politics was a characteristic of inter-war Europe and arose from the economic distress and disillusionment that followed the First World War. Britain was no exception and the cathedral city of Durham had its branch of Mosley's Blackshirts; it seems somewhat inappropriate that they should have their offices under the Young Mens' Christian Association. The Fascists tried to discredit the National Union of Mineworkers and blamed the unions for the distress and unemployment experienced by the north-east in the interwar years. (Durham University Library)

MINERS' DAY, C. 1930. Most of the buildings in the background have gone. The public house was replaced by The Coach and Eight in the late 1960s, the chimney-sweep's house and its neighbours were demolished and later the area became part of the Dunelm Court development. The County Library now occupies the site of the houses below the bridge. The Colpitts family had a long connection with the publican's trade including The Puncheon on this bridge and The Wheatsheaf on Elvet Bridge in 1854, The Griffin Inn in the Market Place in 1894, and Colpitt's Hotel (which still functions) in Colpitt's Terrace in the late 1920s.

LINKED-ARM DANCERS traditionally precede the banners on Miners' Day; the dancers are usually members of mining families rather than the miners themselves. The buildings on the left have been university offices since 1963, the base of Shire Hall, formerly the county's administrative centre, is visible on the upper left. (Durham County Record Office)

MINERS' DAY FUN, c. 1960. It is customary for a few brave souls to dress up for Miners' Day. Here are Popeye and two 'Les Dawson' style women. (Durham County Record Office)

MINERS' DAY CROWDS listening to the speeches on the Racecourse in July 1952. After the speeches miners and their families march with their lodge banners and the bands from the field: some to the cathedral and some home. Others move on to the fair on the adjoining field. This is always well patronized and remains open until midnight. (Dr J.L. Crosby)

THE SPEAKERS at the annual Miners' Gala are usually leading Labour politicians. They stay at the County Hotel in Old Elvet and from its balcony greet the miners' lodges as they march past. Next door to the County and now part of it, was Alderman J.W. Pattison's temperance hotel, the Dunelm. The arch leading to Chapel Passage is visible to the right of the banner; it led to the banks and to an early nineteenth-century Wesleyan chapel, which became a Salvation Army Citadel when the Elvet Methodist Church was built in 1903. At the time when this photograph was taken the building was the alderman's commercial bakery. Chapel and passage were obliterated in the 1970s when the hotel acquired the Pattison property. (Durham County Record Office)

THIS PORTRAIT is the frontispiece to Count Borulawski' *Memoirs* published in 1822; he was only 3 ft 3 in tall, hence the inscription around the picture. From 1820 he lived with the Ebdon family near Prebend's bridge. He was often the object of curiosity. It was said that 'the pitmen would always follow him about, not a little to his annoyance, with open-mouthed amazement, sometimes breaking into hearty oaths of admiration – fascinated by the canny aad man.' In his youth Borulawski met the Empress Maria Theresa who presented him with a ring off the hand of the six-year-old Marie Antoinette, the future Queen of France. He is buried in the cathedral, near the north door; his memorial (by J.A. Cory) is in St Mary-the-Less as it was not allowed in the cathedral.

J.L. MAWSON proudly displays his 1913 motor-bike and the appropriate waterproofs and goggles. (Mrs J. Stobbs)

FIREMEN AT THE CARPET FACTORY of Hugh Mackay Ltd., 5 May 1969. During 1968/9 there were fifteen small, but deliberately-started fires in the premises in Back Lane culminating in the serious one which these men had to face. John Mackay described the scene thus: 'Smoking ruins, fire hoses in all directions, the smell of burning wool, buildings with roofs burnt and open to the sky, looms distorted into unrecognizable shapes – absolute chaos. Workers in little groups – some openly weeping.' (Mr D.V. Kelly)

AN INTERIOR VIEW of Hugh Mackay's Durham carpet factory in Freeman's Place, C. 1930. One of the firm's best-known lines was Yacam, which was almost Mackay spelt backwards. In 1929 the then Prince of Wales (later the uncrowned Edward VIII) worked on a Yacam loom at the North–East Coast Exhibition; the rug containing his efforts was auctioned for the Durham Castle Preservation Fund.

THE WORK-FORCE OF HAUXWELL'S of Atherton Street in 1913. Atherton Street was one of the many streets that were erected under the viaduct after the opening of the railway station in 1857. The street was built by the Durham Co-operative Society and named in honour of Glasgow-born Sir William Atherton (1806–64) who was the MP for Durham from 1852. He supported electoral reform and the removal of all religous disabilities. A lawyer, he served as Judge Advocate of the Fleet, Solicitor-General and Attorney General. G. Hauxwell and Sons was a family firm, well established in Atherton Street before 1873; they were engineers, farriers, millwrights and ironfounders and also owned Crossgate foundry. Many Hauxwell man-hole covers can still be spotted in the city. Mr George Hauxwell is at the extreme right; his son, in the then fashionable Norfolk suit, is at the left of the photograph. (Mrs R.B. Macdonald)

TWO MEN AT WORK in the wheelwright's shop in Atherton Street. At its greatest extent Hauxwell's had another foundry and workshop in Crossgate. (Mrs R.B. Macdonald)

MR HAUXWELL (right) with some of his staff, including Mr Charles Hindmarsh in cap and waistcoat. (Mrs R.B. Macdonald – Mr Hindmarsh's daughter)

A HAUXWELL CELEBRATION in 1969. Mr Jack Hauxwell (left) with Jimmy Henry, Bill Hayes, Alfie Bowes and Charlie Hindmarsh – the longest serving members of staff. (Mrs R.B. Macdonald)

THE KITCHENS OF LUKE'S BAKERY, C. 1965. The business had been founded by Mr Luke's mother Mrs Mary Luke in around 1920 and Mr Luke prided himself on the family character of his business. There were outings and dinners for employees and in later years some of his 'girls' were the daughters of former workers. (Mr J.O. Luke)

WORKERS at Luke's bakery at Bee's Cottage under the viaduct in North Road. Luke's bakery, cake shops and café were well known in the city for over sixty-five years. The bakery centred upon Bee's Cottage, an old house pre-dating the development which was to surround it once the railway was built. Mr John Oliver Luke closed the last shop in 1990. He was descended from two well-known city families. The Olivers had kept the Bridge Hotel and the now vanished Criterion. Luke's café (demolished) in Silver Street was in Sir John Duck's house; Duck's fine staircase is in store and Mr Luke's son has preserved the painting depicting Duck's career. (Mr J.O. Luke)

INSIDE NO. 10 RAVENSWORTH TERRACE. A Japanese parasol disguising the empty grate, the potted parlour palm on a bamboo table, crochet-edged linen, pretty knick-knacks, gas brackets on the wall, large overmantle and heavily-patterned wallpaper – all combine to give an evocative glimpse of a comfortable 1914 drawing-room. (Mrs J. Stobbs)

'MY DEN'. This cosy study for the son of the house, with its books, fancy pipe, photographs and prints gives us a glimpse into a comfortable middle-class home of 1916. (Mrs J. Stobbs)

A FAMILY GROUP taken beside the summer-house in the garden of No. 10 Ravensworth Terrace, 1898. Mr and Mrs Joseph Mawson with their daughters and son Joseph Landt. Two of the girls were to live in the same house for over sixty years. At the time this photograph was taken Mr Mawson's sister, Agnes, was a student at St Hild's College. She too lived in Gilesgate all her life and in the 1960s thoroughly enjoyed thwarting the council's attempts to close the right of way near to her house on Gilesgate Green. In 1950 a desk with 'Agnes Mawson 1898' carved on it was still in use in the university's history department. (Mrs J. Stobbs)

ALL DRESSED UP for a formally posed photograph. Joseph favours 'court dress' while his sisters' outfits suggest a Japanese influence, c. 1897. (Mrs J. Stobbs)

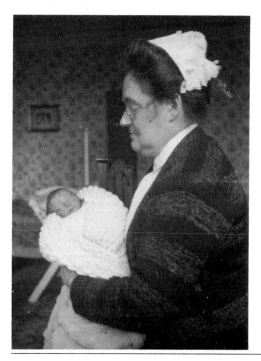

BABY HELEN (a few days old) with Nurse Usher, 1925. Home confinements were the general rule at this time; families who could afford it had resident nurses. New mothers were kept in bed for about twelve days; many nurses recommended them to have their stomachs tightly bound with wet towels as a way of 'keeping their figure'. (Mrs J. Stobbs)

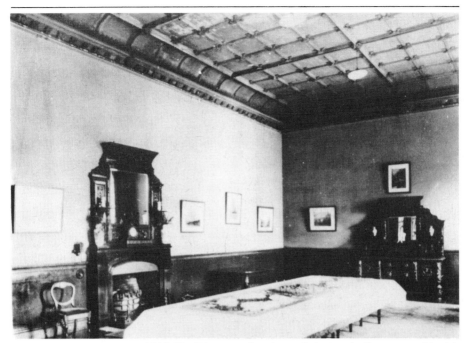

'THE DEAN'S DINING-ROOM', C. 1910. Tradition says that James I slept at the Deanery on his visit to Durham in 1617 when, so the story goes, he complained bitterly about over-new beer.

THE REALITIES OF 'SLUM DWELLINGS NEAR FRAMWELLGATE WATERSIDE' are sharply caught here in this Edis photograph; the outside tap was probably shared with other families. The type of mangle standing in the yard is found now only in museums such as Beamish. Holes in the roof, gaping windows and tattered curtains speak for themselves. (Durham University Library)

A LESSON IN CONVECTION at Durham School; this was taken by 'Jock' – Ian Hay Beith – in 1906. The school moved to its site at Quarryheads in 1844; it began on Palace Green c. 1541 – founded by Henry VIII in the aftermath of the suppresion of the monasteries; there are still King's Scholarships awarded. Durham School is governed by the Dean and Chapter, the 'inheritors' of the monastic foundation which had a grammar and a song school attached to it. So, through these links the school can lay claim to be an early medieval church foundation. (Mrs J. Stobbs)

A WORKERS EDUCATIONAL ASSOCIATION residential course at Hatfield College, 1930s. The photograph was taken behind the now demolished college building which was named Jevons House after Dr F.B. Jevons, who was a great believer in 'extension courses' and did much to develop the extra-mural work of the university. He held 'working men's classes' in a room over a shop on Framwellgate Bridge for many years. Due to his initiative regular residential WEA courses were held at Hatfield from 1922 until the outbreak of war in 1939. (Durham University Library)

THE KITCHEN OF THE JOHNSTON GRAMMAR SCHOOL. Regarded, quite rightly, as a model kitchen at the time, this illustration shows how dramatically kitchen design has changed in the past forty years. (Durham County Record Office)

CURTAIN-CALL after a school play at Durham High School, c. 1965. For most of us amateur dramatics at school are an enjoyable part of extra-curricular activities; for some, it becomes an adult interest. For a few, however, (such as Rowan Atkinson of the Chorister School and Wendy Craig of Durham High), school plays are a prelude to professional careers. Diana Hardcastle (fourth from the left at the back) also entered the theatre and has appeared in television comedy and been a member of the Royal Shakespeare Company. The two 'gallant officers' are Penny Kohnstam and Susan Barker; kneeling centre front is Alison Crosby.

STANGERS CIRCUS comes to town, c. 1895. The circus usually camped on Parson's Field at Elvet Head, 'where in summer a huge circus is often pitched, leaving for the rest of the year a brown circle, like a Brobdingnagian fairy ring.' A ceremonial entrance into the town to drum up custom was also usual and certainly they attracted a goodly crowd along the cobbled street of Old Elvet. This photograph also shows the County Hotel before its façade was stuccoed and the property beyond before its front was commercialized. But the most interesting point about the buildings concerns those on the right for they are the houses demolished when the Shire Hall was begun in 1896. Unfortunately they are in shadow. They include the 'fine house and grounds belonging to Dr Thomas Barron and some adjoining cottages.'

THE HORSE FAIR in Old Elvet, c. 1915. Originally there were four horse fairs a year, of which that on the last Friday in March was the most important as it lasted three days and attracted dealers from a very wide area including Ireland. The fairs moved down to Elvet Green from the Market Place in the late nineteenth century. September 1915 was said to have seen the worst fair on record due to the demands of the army, but the fairs survived both world wars. They faded away in the mid-1950s, by which time the dealers were mostly 'travellers'. The author can remember them putting their ponies through their paces in 1953 in front of these very houses and sealing a deal by a handshake just as the two men at the right are doing. (Durham University Library)

A SUMMER MEETING of the Architectural and Archaeological Society of Durham and Northumberland – 'Arc. and Arc.' to its friends, c. 1913. Joseph Mawson (with stick) is sitting in the front row; his daughter, Anna, is behind him. On the back of the picture other people are named: on the front row Mrs Raine; on the second row, Mrs W. Gray; on the third row, Mrs Percy, Mr Goodyear, Mrs Alf Smith, Mr L. Gradon; and at the back Mr W. Smith, P. Waite, Mr Picton, T. Parry, M. Fowler, Mr Lowes, Mr Potts, Alf Smith, and Mr and Mrs Mohun. Summer meetings are still organized by the society. (Mrs J. Stobbs)

SLEDGING DOWN RAVENSWORTH TERRACE, c. 1910. The backs of Nos 210–25 in lower Gilesgate seen in the background are still clearly recognizable today. (Mrs J. Stobbs)

A PROCESSION down King Street, now always called North Road, c. 1920. The King William IV public house on its prominent corner site and King Street were so called because they both opened in William's coronation year, 1830. The procession appears to be in fancy dress but the occasion has not been identified. More than one copy of the photograph has been seen; one owner believes it to be a chapel party, another the suffragettes, a third, Miner's Day.

THE BRIDGE HOTEL, North Road, was named after the viaduct under which it shelters. The Peverall family, who also farmed at Crook Hall Farm, were early publicans at the Bridge; Elizabeth Peverall held the licence in the 1870s. It passed to Edwin A. Oliver in the 1880s; he also had a small mineral-water factory. By the time of the First World War Edwin's son was publican and Edwin had three tobacconist shops. After the war Henry Robertson was the publican. Mr J.O. Luke's mother was an Oliver and she had a confectioner's next door to the Bridge. (Mr J.O. Luke)

DURHAM CITY RUGBY FOOTBALL CLUB'S third team – cup finalists of 1925/6. Front row, left to right: L. Jackson; W. Trotter; J. Smurthwaite; and W. Martin. Middle row: J. Malpas, trainer; J.O. Luke; E. Hodgeson; L. Todd; R. Alderson; W. Malpas; P. Hodgeson; and coach, J. Hauxwell. In the back row: A. Hearn; G.F. Alderson; R. Birch; P. Reed; W. Hay; W.V. Carpenter; J. Todd; and W. Driver. The trainer's grandson was the team's mascot. (Mr J.O. Luke)

DURHAM ROWING CLUB, c. 1930. In front of the crossed oars stand Ralph Powney and J. Hopper, in between J. Veitch, the coach, and H.M. Coyne, the president (on the right). J. Shawcross and Bob Powney sit beside the club's trophies, with the cox in front. (Mr J.O. Luke)

MR A.O. PIGG on the steps of the Town Hall with local scouts and the mayor and her husband, the Revd R. Thornhill. Mr Pigg had just received his warrant as District Commissioner of Scouts at an inter-denominational St George's Day service held in the Town Hall. The service was also a memorial service to Professor J.A. Chalmers. 'Skip' Chalmers had been district commissioner for many years and was a well-known figure in the Scouting movement. (Mrs M.A. Thornhill)

BOOTS LENDING LIBRARY, Silver Street, c. 1950. The library was an unexpected oasis of quiet in the busy street; its large window offered a sweeping view across the river to Framwellgate and the railway station, and held some pleasant heraldic stained glass. When it first opened a book could be borrowed for a week at a cost of 3d.; later the rate was increased to 6d. (Durham University Library)

GREY COLLEGE created the winning float of the March 1967 Rag Week procession with their 'Woman Machine'. A variety of ingredients fed into the machine produced 'real live women'. (Mrs M.A. Thornhill)

SECTION SIX

Changing Durham

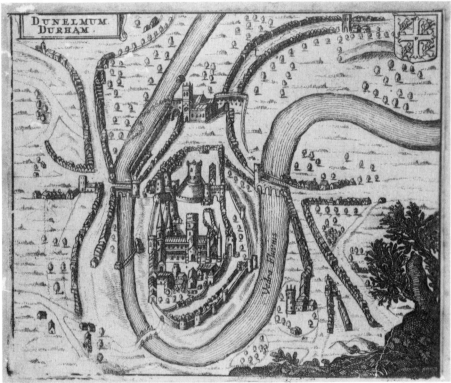

MUCH OF THE CITY recorded by Matthew Pattison in 1595 remains: the great loop of the River Wear; the peninsular complex dominated by the cathedral and castle; the river crossings of Framwellgate; Elvet and the Prebends; the Market Place with St Nicholas'; the other parish churches of St Giles, St Margaret and St Oswald. All are with us still. The main streets are clearly shown – the Baileys, Old and New Elvet, South Street, Framwellgate, and Claypath leading into Gilesgate at the leaden cross. A pattern of remarkable continuity emerges which would be recognizable to a pilgrim three centuries before Pattison and to a traveller three centuries after. However, it is a pattern unable to cope with late-twentieth-century needs. Since the mid-sixties, major road and bridge construction and large-scale building development have superimposed a new pattern upon the old. The following photographs, all but four of them by Mr D.V. Kelly, illustrate some of the changes which were designed to adapt a restricted medieval city to modern times.

PART OF GILESGATE, 1962. Sometimes called 'Gilliegat', Gilesgate was the major road east to the ports of Bishop and Monk Wearmouth until the new road was begun in 1967. This photograph shows the Volunteer Arms Hotel (named in honour of the drill hall a few doors below), Cowies motor-bike shop and, beyond the drill hall with its archway leading to Moody's Buildings and the Durham Ox. Magdalene Lane alongside Cowies originally led to the medieval hospital of St Mary Magdalene and, much later, to Durham's first railway station of 1844. The bus stop seen in the middle distance was commonly called 'Porter's', many people thought this was after the grocer's shop which preceded Cowies. In fact Porter's Close is mentioned in seventeenth- and eighteenth-century tithe records, long before the shop was built on it.

EARLY 1960s. The new road carving its way eastwards through the obliterated Co-operative Terrace towards the new Milburngate Bridge. Behind the plain Georgian façade of the rear of Market Hall is St Nicholas' Church with its bold spire. Alongside St Nicholas' is a fragment of Old Walkergate. The spire (middle left) is that of the United Reform Church of 1885–6 built by H.T. Gradon. Near it, a block of office accommodation with shops beneath; outwardly the buildings demolished to make way for this block were late-nineteenth- and twentieth-century. Demolition revealed evidence of much earlier building, including an early-seventeenth-century staircase. In the middle foreground Milburngate House is still in its initial stage. Old buildings to its left await demolition prior to the second stage of building. In summer a remainder of Co-operative Terrace still appears – lupins flower on the north bank of the now completed road at this spot – a legacy from the gardens of the vanished houses.

ABANDONED SHOPS in lower Claypath await demolition and look down upon the demolition of Walkergate (c. 1967). Only St Nicholas' now remains. The steps leading down beside the west end of the church are said to be the place where Archbishop Wickwane ran out of the city in 1283 to escape pursuing townsfolk by taking refuge in Kepier Hospital; he had incurred their anger by attempting to interfere in the affairs of the Cathedral Monastery. Walkergate led down to the Durham carpet factory and provided a convenient corner where the market stalls were stacked away forty years ago. A disused factory building became the Palace Theatre in the late nineteenth cnetury and later a cinema, known a little unkindly in the 1940s as the 'Flea Pit'. Charlie Chaplin performed in the Palace Theatre as a Lancashire laddie very early in his career.

OLD FRAMWELLGATE leading to Aykley Heads and County Hall, c. 1967. This is the road down which James VI of Scotland was escorted by the burgesses of Durham in 1603 when he was on his way to London to become James I of England. It looks like a rural retreat in a quiet backwater but the bulldozer and excavations visible on the left show early beginnings of the transformation of the old Framwellgate Peth into the modern dual carriageway which now occupies the site.

A VIEW OF DURHAM from the railway station. Old Milburngate is in the foreground with the (sham) half-timbered façade of The Blue Bell and behind it the terraced housing in Sidegate. Beyond, work on Milburngate House and the new bridge has just begun; a temporary works site has been set up below the Market Hall. On the left is the somewhat forlorn mid-eighteenth-century façade of a former Roman Catholic convent in Castle Chare. Opposite are the council houses erected in the 1930s. One row was called Lovegreen Street after a local family who for three generations rowed people across the Horsehole (roughly the site of Milburngate Bridge). Although the service had long been discontinued, the writer had the experience of being rowed across in 1948 and paid the customary fee of 2d.

THE SAME VIEW IN 1975/6. The council houses have gone, Milburngate House is open; Milburngate Bridge and the first stage of Milburngate shopping precinct have been completed. The former convent in Castle Chare, with its fine eighteenth-century internal plaster-work survives, much improved. The problem of cars within the city is grave. Any open space and the cars move in — as this photograph clearly demonstrates.

THE BUILDING of this fine, if assertive, railway viaduct and station of 1857 encouraged the building of many terraces of houses such as Lambton Street. Some survive, but others, as these around the former top of North Road, were cleared away before the building of the new roundabout. The intrusion of shop-fronts into what was originally built as a terrace of houses indicates the increasing commercial development in North Road in the late nineteenth and twentieth century.

LOOKING UP GILESGATE'S SECOND BANK in the 1950s. The ancient street still had its cobbled sets which were removed in 1955. The raised pavement on the right leads past the lodge of the Manor House and up to Belvedere, the prominent early-eighteenth-century house. Both were formerly owned by the Marquess of Londonderry; Manor House is properly so-called as it was built on land allocated to the Londonderrys as Lords of the Manor in the Gilesgate Inclosure Act of 1816. Belvedere ('beautiful view') is now a hostel for university students.

CLAYPATH WAS THE AREA most adversely affected by road schemes. The demolition of lower Claypath (shown here in 1963) isolated the shops further up the street from the shopping 'flow' in the market area, of which Claypath had been a natural extension. The upper storeys of many shops, notably Timothy Whites, here show that they were once fine and substantial town-houses. Next to Whites is Norman Richardson's former travel agency. Mr Richardson was a notable Mayor of Durham in 1964, and is still prominent in business and tourist circles. Beyond is Fred Robinson's pork shop; people came from miles around for his delicious pork and home-made sausages.

ALL HAVE GONE (apart from St Nicholas', extreme left) as this photograph shows.

THE WATERLOO HOTEL, named in honour of the famous battle, had a commanding position looking up New Elvet (the half-timbered treatment is post 1900). Next to it are the fine County Courts of 1871 designed by Soulby in early Tudor style, mostly of Waskerley Fell marble. This photograph, taken during the severe winter of 1964, shows the junction of New and Old Elvet, near the approach to Elvet Bridge. In medieval times the present Old Elvet lay in the Borough of Elvet, while New Elvet lay in the Barony of Elvet. 'New' Elvet is the older street, and was so called Old Elvet when the new Elvet was opened up. In the fifteenth century, however, they exchanged names.

A NEW VISTA was opened up by demolition in the late 1960s as shown in this photograph looking across the new Elvet Bridge (1975) towards the rear of Claypath. The spire is that of the former Presbyterian church in Claypath, now the United Reform church.

A VIEW ACROSS THE RIVER from the corner of Framwellgate Bridge looking towards the railway viaduct and station (on the skyline). On the left of St Godric's Roman Catholic Church designed by E.W. Pugin (1864 and tower added 1909–10) is the Presbytery House, the former Roman Catholic convent and late Victorian School. The end of Lambton Walk obtrudes on the left.

THE NEW TOWN HOUSES on the riverside echo the style of the vanished terrace houses, while the open view looking towards St Godric's has been all but obliterated by the Milburngate shopping precinct (1972–76 by the Building Design Partnership).

MILBURNGATE HOUSE, housing the offices of the National Savings Bank and DHSS, protrudes defiantly into the Durham City landscape.

THE ADDITION OF THE SECOND PHASE of the Milburngate shopping precinct has lessened the impact of Milburngate House but further accentuates the contrast of style and type of development to be seen on the different sides of the river. In the foreground, the old-style Durham – small-scale, piecemeal and local development; on the other bank the large scale planned development of the later twentieth century.

YOUNG ANDREW KELLY grins mischievously at his father photographing a scene familiar to Durham students and residents for over 130 years – a crew practising on the river below Elvet Bridge and the coach giving advice (or worse) as they rest their oars. The numbers on the arches of the bridge are for the benefit of oarsmen during regattas. Brown's boat-house overhanging the river is also part and parcel of the Durham river scene. The hint of changes to come is given in the new Halifax Building Society building on the other side of Elvet Bridge.

THE BUILDING OF THE NEW ELVET BRIDGE in 1976 made a very obvious change to the peaceful scene, but once completed did not affect enjoyment of boating on the river.

ATHERTON STREET was part of the terrace development which followed the opening of the present Durham railway station. The building at the end is Hauxwell's former iron foundry. William Robson, a mason who worked on St Godric's, lived on one side of the foundry during the 1870s and George Hauxwell on the other. The demolition of this row certainly showed the fine arches of the viaduct to greater effect.

Below, right:
CHANGE OFTEN MEETS RESISTANCE simply because it is change. The developments within Durham City during the past twenty-five years have not pleased everyone and some have mistakenly assumed that an ancient city untouched by time and change has suddenly been faced by overwhelming changes. This is not so. The largely nineteenth-century façades around the Five Ways Hotel on the west end of Framwellgate Bridge hid within them traces of much earlier building, including this unexpected gem, the remains of a fourteenth-century timber-framed house with late fifteenth-century additions at the rear. The council's decision to retain and restore it *in situ* was highly commendable, and it can now be admired in its restored state by shoppers entering the Milburngate shopping precinct.

THE WEST SIDE of New Elvet is now dominated by three university developments – Dunelm House and the Riverside lecture blocks I and II. Here, the site for Dunelm House is being surveyed. Behind are Fowler's salesrooms, where a wide variety of goods was auctioned with firmness interlaced with humour by the late Mr Matthew Fowler, whose family business had begun in Saddler Street. Behind the salesrooms may be seen a small inter-war council-house development where the possibilities of using the cathedral view were hardly considered by the architect.

MASONS THE CHEMISTS, in Silver Street, was also an old building with a hidden earlier history. The praiseworthy interest of the developers and the sensitivity of the architects, Rooker, Stringer and Jones, have resulted in layers of history being revealed.

BEHIND THE OUTWARDLY NINETEENTH-CENTURY SHOP-FRONT was a timber-framed building of around 1560, with hints of a still earlier building. Inside, generations of plaster and paint have been removed to reveal the hidden past of a building which once belonged to the chantry chapels on Elvet Bridge and has since had many different occupants and owners, some local, some London-based.

THE CATHEDRAL from near Prebends Bridge, c. 1947. This is the view so beloved of artists and photographers – the cathedral towers rising above the steep, wooded banks with the old Fulling Mill nestling by the river below. Reproduced here by permission of Mr G. Lye, the compiler's copy was purchased for 1s. when she was a student. It emphasizes the undisturbed serenity of the essential Durham.

ACKNOWLEDGEMENTS

Acknowledgement must be made to the following who generously made photographs available for inclusion in this collection of photographs of the City of Durham:

Mr D.V. Kelly, for his very special contribution

Mrs J. Stobbs, for access to her father's albums • Revd and Mrs R. Thornhill, for illustrations of a mayor's year • Mrs N. Macdonald, for access to her family album • Mr D. Jones, for photographs from his professional records

Mr J.O. Luke, for information and photographs • Mr S. Dean and Mr I. Nelson of Durham County Library • Miss J. Gill and Durham County Record Office Durham University Library – Miss E. Rainey and Mr R. Norris • Durham City Planning Department

Their cheerful and patient cooperation was sincerely appreciated. Photographs whose ownership is not given are from the compiler's own collection.